ANALECTA BIBLICA
INVESTIGATIONES SCIENTIFICAE IN RES BIBLICAS

——————————— 115 ———————————

STEPHEN FRANCIS MILETIC

"ONE FLESH": EPH. 5.22-24, 5.31
MARRIAGE AND THE NEW CREATION

EDITRICE PONTIFICIO ISTITUTO BIBLICO – ROMA 1988

ISBN 88-7653-115-7

EDITRICE PONTIFICIA UNIVERSITÀ GREGORIANA
EDITRICE PONTIFICIO ISTITUTO BIBLICO
Piazza della Pilotta, 35 - 00187 Roma

For Joyce Elaine (Bachmeier) Miletic

ACKNOWLEDGMENTS

It is with pleasure that I acknowledge my debt of gratitude to many friends who supported this study in one way or another. I am especially indebted to Fr. R. A. Wild, S.J., who worked with me as my dissertation director. To Fr. D.A. Keefe, S.J., Fr. W.S. Kurz, S.J., Dr. J.J. Schmitt and Dr. R.A. Edwards, I owe an acknowledgment of debt to their kindness, critical reading and human support offered to me while this project was at the dissertation stage.

I offer sincere and grateful thanks to the many patrons who offered spiritual and material support for this study. A special thanks to Mr. Michael Power for his generous and kind assistance in preparing the indices.

Without the love, understanding, selflessness, compassion, good humor, and total support of Joyce, Isaac-Francis, Heather-Ann, and more recently, Rose-Sharon, the unreasonable demands academia has made on my family would have been unbearable. It is with gratitude, respect, admiration and deep affectionate love that I dedicate this study to Joyce.

14 September, 1986   Stephen Francis Miletic
Feast of the Trimph of the Cross   Nepean, Canada

Contents

Abbreviations

AB	Anchor Bible
AnBib	Analecta Biblica
ASNU	Acta seminarii neotestamentici upsaliensis
Bib	*Biblica*
BZNW	Beiheft zur ZNW
CWK	LiberLäromedel Lund
EKKNT	Evangelisch-Katholischer Kommentar zum Neuen Testament
ErJb	*Eranos Jahrbuch*
ExpTim	*Expository Times*
FRLANT	Forschungen zur Religion und Literatur des Alten und Neuen Testaments
HNTC	Harper's NT Commentaries
HTKNT	Herders theologischer Kommentar zum Neuen Testament
HTR	*Harvard Theological Review*
IDBSup	Supplementary volume to G.A. Buttrick (ed.) *Interpreter's Dictionary of the Bible*
ICC	International Critical Commentary
JAAR	*Journal of the American Academy of Religion*
JBL	*Journal of Biblical Literature*
JSNT	*Journal for the Study of the New Testament*
JTS	*Journal of Theological Studies*
MNTC	Moffatt NT Commentary
NCB	New Century Bible
NTC	New Testament Commentaries
NTS	*New Testament Studies*
NovT	*Novum Testamentum*
OJRS	*Ohio Journal of Religious Studies*
QD	*Quaestiones disputatae*
RB	*Revue biblique*
Semeia	*An Experimental Journal for Biblical Criticism*
SBLDS	SBL Dissertation Series
SBLMS	SBL Monograph Series
SBLSBS	SBL Sources for Biblical Study
ScEs	*Science et Esprit*
SNTSMS	Society for New Testament Studies Monograph Series
TLZ	*Theologische Literaturzeitung*

TDNT   G. Kittel and G. Griedrich (eds.), *Theological Dictionary of the New Testament*

WMANT   Wissenschaftliche Monographien zum Alten und Neuen Testament

WPC   Westminster Pelican Commentaries

ZNW   *Zeitschrift für die neutestamentliche Wissenschaft*

ZRGG   *Zeitschrift für Religions- und Geistesgeschichte*

CHAPTER I.

Introduction

A. Introduction

The address to wives at Eph. 5.22-24 is deceptively simple. The text informs us that wives ought to be subordinate to their own husbands (v. 22) because the husband is "head" of the wife just as Christ is "head" of the church (v. 23); just as the church is subordinate to Christ, so must wives be subordinate to their husbands in everything (v. 24). Nothing could seem more straightforward: the passage calls for the subordination of the wife to the husband in everything. That the author exhorts Christian wives to be subordinate is beyond dispute. However, what such an exhortation to wives meant in first century Mediterranean culture is far from clear. Attempts to ascertain what this passage communicated make the complexities of the text apparent.

For example, the author *never* applies the verb ὑποτάσσω ("to subordinate") directly to the wife (cf. Eph. 5.22, 24b)! Stated positively, the author applies the verb *only* to the church (cf. 5.24a). The complexity of this text continues to unfold when we note that the author justifies the injunction by means of christological (5.22: "as to the Lord"; 5.23b: "Christ is head of the church"), soteriological (5.23c: "he, savior of the body") and ecclesiological (5.24a: "and as the church is subordinate to Christ") elements.

Further degrees of complexity emerge when we note that Ephesians contains and interprets a variety of traditions. Almost twenty years ago E. Käsemann pointed out the mosaic-like quality of Ephesians, emphasizing the creative integration and synthesis of ideas accomplished by the author[1]. Numerous studies link the text of Ephesians to biblical traditions,[2] Philo,[3] Qumran,[4] other Jewish traditions,[5] and to the Pauline

---

[1] See "Ephesians and Acts," *Studies in Luke-Acts*, eds. L.E. KECK, et. al. (Nashville: Abingdon Press, 1966), p. 288.

[2] Of the many studies that could be listed, see E. PERCY, *Der Leib Christi in den paulinischen Homologomena und Antilogomena* (Lund: Universitets Arsschrift, 1942); S. HANSON, *The Unity of the Church in the New Testament, Colossians and Ephesians*, ASNU 14 (Uppsala: Almquist, 1946); F. MUSSNER, *Christus, Das All und die Kirche: Studien zum Theologie des Epheserbriefes*, Trier Theologische Studien 5 (Trier: Paulinus Verlag, 1955).

[3] C. COLPE, "Zur Leib-Christi-Verstellung im Epheserbrief," in *Judentum, Christ-*

Corpus.[6] Most recognize the unquestionably close relationship between Ephesians and Colossians.[7] J. Paul Sampley's work provides the first systematic study which traces specific traditions incorporated in Eph. 5.22-33.[8] Of all the points of contact between Eph. 5.22-33 and its possible sources, most would agree that the relationship between Ephesians and Colossians is exceptional. It is generally accepted that the degree and number of verbal parallels between these two epistles outranks those between Ephesians and other possible parallels.[9] The points of contact between the *Haustafeln* or household codes of Col. 3.18-4.2 and Eph. 5.22-6.9 is a matter of record.[10]

---

entum, Kirche, ed. W. Eltester, BZNW 26 (Berlin: Töpelmann, 1960); E. BRANDENBURGER, *Adam und Christus*, WMANT 7 (Neukirchen: Neukirchener Verlag, 1962); D.C. SMITH, *Jewish and Greek Traditions in Ephesians 2:11-22* (Ph.D. dissertation, Yale University, 1970); *idem*, "The Two Made One: Some Obsevations on Eph. 2.14-18," *OJRS* 1 (1973):34-54.

[4] See K.G. KUHN, "Der Epheserbrief im Lichte der Qumrantexte," *NTS* 7 (1961):334-346.

[5] Connections between Ephesians and Jewish apocalypticism have been suggested by E. SCHWEIZER, "Die Kirche als Leib Christi in den paulinischen Antilegomena," *TLZ* 86 (1961):241-256.

[6] C.L. MITTON has arranged the point of contact between Ephesians and the rest of the Pauline Corpus throughout his *The Epistle to the Ephesians: Its Authorship, Origin and Purpose* (Oxford: The Clarendon Press, 1951) (hereafter cited as *Ephesians*).

[7] See MITTON, *Ephesians*, "Appendix I," pp. 280 ff., for parallels between Ephesians and Colossians. See also J. COUTTS, "The Relationship of Ephesians and Colossians." *NTS* 4 (1958):201-207; W. MUNRO, "Col. iii. 18-iv.1 and Eph. v.21-vi.9: Evidence of a Late Literary Stratum?" *NTS* 18 (1972):434-447.

[8] See *And the Two Shall Become One Flesh. A Study of Traditions in Ephesians*, SNTSMS 16 (Cambridge: Cambridge University Press, 1971), pp. 16-76.

[9] E.g., MITTON, *Ephesians*, pp. 57-60. This kind similarity has led a number of scholars to suggest that rather than postulating a common source from which both authors drew, it is more suggest that rather than postulating a common source from which both authors drew, it is more correct to suggest that one document depended heavily on the other for its structure and part of its content.

[10] See SAMPLEY, *One Flesh*, pp. 17-25 for a discussion of this point. See J.E. CROUCH, *The Origin and Intention of the Colossian Haustafel*, FRLANT 109 (Göttingen: Vandenhoeck und Ruprecht, 1972) for a discussion of the *Haustafel* or household code in Antiquity. See Sampley, Ibid., pp. 18-30, for a discussion of the *Haustafel* form and its development within Pauline tradition. See D.L. BALCH, *Let Wives be Submissive: The Domestic Code in 1 Peter*, SBLMS 26 (Chico, CA: Scholars Press, 1981), pp. 23-62 for a recent treatment of *Haustafel* traditions in Antiquity. The position that Eph. 5.22-24 represents an expansion of the Colossian *Haustafel* generally presupposes the pseudepigraphical nature of Ephesians. The arguments of this study do not depend on whether or not Ephesians is pseudepigraphic. At the present time my tendency is to think that if Ephesians is not from Paul, then it is "authentically Pauline" in the sense that it is a significant interpretation of Pauline ideas which does not betray Paul's genuine insights. For systematic treatments and a litany of arguments for and against Pauline authorship see W. HENDRIKSEN, *Exposition of Ephesians*, NTC 2 (Grand Rapids, Mich.: Baker Book House, 1967), pp. 32-55. T.K. ABBOTT, *A Critical and Exegetical Commentary on*

Let me illustrate the close relationship between the address to wives at Eph. 5.22-24 and Col. 3.18 with the following example. The text of Col. 3.18 reads, αἱ γυναῖκες ὑποτάσσεσθε τοῖς ἀνδράσιν ὡς ἀνῆκεν ἐν κυρίῳ.[11] The italicized portions of Eph. 5.22 indicate the modifications, αἱ γυναῖκες [*ellipsis of the verb*] τοῖς ἰδίοις ἀνδράσιν ὡς τῷ κυρίῳ.[12] The author of Ephesians deletes the verb, adds ἰδίοις ("your own") and replaces ἀνῆκεν ἐν κυρίῳ ("as is fitting in the Lord") with τῷ κυρίῳ ("to the Lord"). The remainder of the address to wives, Eph. 5.23-24, represents the author's expansion of the *Haustafel* tradition inherited from Col. 3.18.

Because the author of Ephesians radically modifies the address to wives which he drew from Col. 3.18 (1) by not applying the verb directly to the wife and (2) by incorporating christological, soteriological and ecclesiological elements into the address to wives, the key to understanding how the author of Ephesians incorporates traditional materials within the address to wives (and husbands) is dependent on the way he has modified Col. 3.18-19. In addition, such an approach alerts us to the nuance given to the address to wives at Eph. 5.22-24. To restate the original question: Precisely what does the exhortation at Eph. 5.22-24 demand of the Christian wife within the context of first century Mediterranean culture?

Almost one hundred years ago the issue of what Eph. 5.22-24 may have intended was not the critical exegetical question it is today. Even with the advent of the suffrage movement, women (not just wives) were still generally thought of as subordinate (and therefore inferior) to men. T.K. Abbott's still valuable commentary comes from an age when extensive knowledge of the Greek and Latin Fathers, of the great Reformation and Counter-Reformation commentators, exacting grammatical analysis and textual criticism formed the basic cadre of the accomplished exegete. His commentary also comes from a cultural climate which presupposed the understanding that wives were subordinate to their husbands. Sociology of knowledge centered on questions of church authority, the hermeneutical relationship between knowledge of the sciences (i.e., *Wissenschaft*) and faith — all of this within Protestant

---

the Epistles to the Ephesians and to the Colossians, ICC (Edinburgh: T. & T. Clark [1897], 1979), pp. ix-xxiii; more recently A. VAN ROON, *The Authorship of Ephesians*, Trans. S. Proscod-Jokel (Leiden: C.J. Brill, 1979) and M. BARTH, *Ephesians*, AB 34-34A, (Garden City, N.Y.: Doubleday & Company, 1974), pp. 36-50. All of the above argue that Ephesians is from Paul. Against the above I find cogent the cumulative arguments presented by Mitton, see the internal evidence he provides in *Ephesians*, "Chapter XIX."

[11] The RSV reads, "Wives be subordinate to your husbands as is fitting in the Lord."

[12] My translation reads, "Wives [*ellipsis of the verb*], to your *own* husbands as *to the Lord*."

and Catholic communities clearly controlled by *men*.[13] Exegetes did not examine how their own views of women influenced their interpretation of women in the first century. It therefore comes as no surprise to learn that Abbott does not address the verb "to subordinate" as this relates to the wife. All we have is his summary of 5.22-33, where he translates the wife's subordination in terms of her being "subject" to the husband.[14] The situation remained largely unchanged during the first few decades of this century.[15]

The advent of the most recent women's movement in the 1960's prompted many to re-examine basic presuppositions about the roles of women in the church, the business and political communities, the economy and the family. Within the past two decades the question of the wife's subordination has been reopened on personal, religious institutional and academic levels of reflection. Studies of Ephesians within this period manifest profound differences of opinion as to what the text meant in the first century A.D., and what it could mean today.

Whether scholars ascribe a negative or positive value to the injunction for subordination at Eph. 5.22-24, there is general agreement about the social world of Ephesians, even if its specific *Sitz im Leben* is still an unsolved problem. The argument proposed by most is as follows.[16] It is not surprising that the text of Eph. 5.22-24 exhorts wives to be subordinate since such an exhortation coupled with the hierarchical family structure of husband-over-wife was a widespread social structure of the Roman Empire in the first century A.D.

This line of thinking correctly notes that such an exhortation is neither unique nor uncommon prior to and after the advent of Christianity. Classical Greek philosophers discussed not just the subordination of women but the obedience of children and slaves as these intersected with questions of human nature (i.e., ruler and ruled), justice in the city-state and household management.[17] Such discussions were very much alive in

---

[13] For a convenient survey of such questions see P. STUHLMACHER, *Historical Criticism and Theological Interpretation of Scripture*, Trans. R.A. Harrisville (Philadelphia: Fortress Press, 1977), pp. 41-60.

[14] See *Ephesians*, p. 165.

[15] For example, see J.A. ROBINSON, *St. Paul's Epistle to the Ephesians*[2] (London: J. Clarke & Co. Ltd., 1922), p. 124.

[16] I shall examine particular arguments on both side of the question below. What follows is simply a sketch of the parameters of the debate.

[17] For a recent discussion of the social world of the household relative to the Pauline tradition see W.A. MEEKS, *The First Urban Christians: The Social World of the Apostle Paul* (New Haven/London: Yale University Press, 1983). A reconstruction of the social network of household relationships is found on pp. 75-77. Meeks points out that all women were not treated in the same fashion. Those of the upper classes had more social and other kinds of independence (pp. 23-25). He is correct to note that the *dominant* pattern of family relationships was hierarchical and patriarchal (p. 76).

Greco-Roman circles at the advent of Christianity.[18] Even if the basis of its understanding of women differs radically from the debates in Greek philosophy, and, granted that in the first century A.D. Judaism was not a homogeneous religious tradition,[19] first century Jewish traditions express similar attitudes toward women. Its many perceptions of the woman/wife were filtered through common patriarchal settings which understood her as being subordinate to males — be they fathers, husbands or even brothers.[20] That is, the image of Christian marriage represented at Eph. 5.22-24 is seen to overlap with Greco-Roman and Jewish social systems which were, for the most part, patriarchal. Even the subordination of the church to Christ (Eph. 5.24) manifests sociological patterns of first century Asia Minor. In short, the text of Eph. 5.22-24 articulates a widely held value system which expected subordination of wives to their own husbands.

It is after this first methodological step that scholarship on Ephesians parts ways. When the text of Eph. 5.22-24 is compared to the undisputed letters of Paul, some scholars view the injunction for subordination as a regression away from egalitarian male/female relationships thought to be expressed in such Pauline texts as Gal. 3.28.[21] In this instance, a Pauline text in seen as standing *against* its culture while Eph. 5.22-24 is seen as standing *with* its culture. Let me illustrate with some examples.

R. Scroggs takes the baptismal formula at Gal. 3.28 as an indication

---

[18] See BALCH, *Let Wives be Submissive*, pp. 44-45 a for a summary of how the discussion of these topics was still alive in the first century B.C.

[19] One need only compare the messianic expectations of the the Pharisees, the Samaritans, the Qumran community and Jesus of Nazareth for this to be clear.

[20] I do not wish to imply that Jewish traditions had nothing good to say about women; see the books of Ruth, Esther and Judith. See also B.J. BROOTEN, *Women Leaders in the Ancient Synagogues: Inscriptional Evidence and Background Issues*, Brown Judaic Series 36 (Chico, C.A.: Scholars Press, 1982), who argue that nineteen Greek and Latin inscriptions which ascribe leadership roles to women indicate that during the Roman and Byzantine periods women served in leadership positions in a number of synagogues in Africa, Asia Minor, Crete, Egypt, Greece, Palestine and so on. It is impossible to rehearse evidence illustrating how women and wives were viewed and treated within various first century A.D. Jewish traditions; see K.H. Rengstorf, "Mann un Frau im Urchristentum," in *Arbeitsgemeinschaft für Forschung des Landes Nordrhein-Westfalen*, Geisteswissenschaften 12 (Cologne/Oplanden: Westdeutscher, 1954) pp. 7-52; J. LEIPOLDT, *Die Frau in der antiken, Welt und im Urchristentum* (Gütersloh, 1962); a more recent treatment of this question can be found in G. DAUTZENBURG, et. al., *Die Frau im Urchristentum*, QD 95 (Freiburg/Basel/Wein: Herder, 1983). In addition, I do not assume that Jewish Palestinian culture was removed from Greco-Roman culture, see M. HENGEL, *Judaism and Hellenism*, 2 vols. (Philadelphia: Fortress Press, 1974), pp. 83-106.

[21] The RSV reads, "There is neither Jew nor Greek, there is neither slave nor free, there is neither male nor female, for you are all one in Christ Jesus."

of the equality between women and men within Pauline communities during Paul's lifetime.[22] He writes:

> Contrary to the position of subordination in which women generally lived in first-century Mediterranean culture, the position they discovered in the early Christian communities was one of acceptance and, particularly in the earliest decades, equality.[23]

That is, the early Pauline tradition evidences equality between women and men, wives and husbands.[24] If the early Christian communities were powerless to alter the outside culture, later Pauline interpretations of women and wives, evidenced perhaps at 1 Cor. 14.33b-35 but certainly at Eph. 5.22-24 and 1 Tim. 2.11-12, seem to have fallen into the temptation of completely accepting first century Mediterranean cultural "valuatians" by exhorting the wife to be subordinate. In effect later Pauline tradition, esp. Eph. 5.22-24, is thought to mirror patriarchal values by demanding the wife's subordination to the husband. Scroggs is not alone in this interpretation.[25] E. Schüssler Fiorenza's analysis of Eph. 5.22 leads her to suggest that the injunction for subordination "reinforces the patriarchal marriage pattern and justifies it christologically."[26] She differs from Scroggs by recognizing that the injunction to love the wife (given three times to the husband, 5.25, 28, 33) represents a significant modification of the Colossian address to husbands (Col. 3.19) and a radical challenge to patriarchal domination. Nevertheless, her view of subordination is still quite negative:

> this christological modification of the husband's patriarchal position and duties does not have the power, theologically, to transform the patriarchal pattern of the household code, even though this might have been the intention of the author.[27]

---

[22] See his "Women in the N.T.," *IDBSup*, pp. 966-968, esp. p. 966.

[23] Ibid. See also his "Paul and the Eschatological Woman," *JAAR* XL (1972):283-303.

[24] Scroggs (Ibid.) points to 1 Cor. 7 as another illustration of equality, this time between wives and husbands.

[25] I cannot survey all of the literature representing this approach, which by this date is legion. For one of the earliest illustrations of this point of view see the the essay by the former Dean of Harvard Divinity School, now Bishop of Stockholm, K. STENDAHL, *The Bible and the Role of Women. A Case Study in Hermeneutics*, Trans. E.T. Sander, Facet Books, Biblical Series 15 (Philadelphia: Fortress Press, 1966). More recently see W.O. WALKER, Jr., "The 'Theology of Women's Place' and the 'Paulinist' Tradition," *Semeia* 28 (1983):101-112.

[26] See *In Memory of Her: A Feminist Theological Reconstruction of Christian Origins* (New York: Crossroad, 1983), p. 269.

[27] Ibid., p. 270.

In her interpretation, the exhortation to the whole community at 5.21 ("Be subject to one another in the fear of Christ") is "spelled out for the Christian wife as requiring submission and inequality."[28] That is, "Ephesians christologically cements the inferior position of the wife in the marriage relationship."[29]

I would agree with two points. First, there is no doubt that the injunction to love as Christ loves (Eph. 5.25) is a serious challenge to patriarchal domination in marriage. Second, I would agree that such a radical challenge does not directly alter the injunction for subordination. However, the injunction to the husband does indirectly alter the wife's subordination because now she is called to be subordinate to a love that is Christ-like and therefore not self-serving. Even so, Fiorenza's fundamental point still stands — the injunction to love does not directly alter what appears to be a clear perpetuation of a patriarchal pattern which associates women with a subordinate and inferior role in marriage. Perhaps the counterpart to the transformation of the husband's role may be in the church/wife analogy at Eph. 5.24, as I shall argue later in this study.

J.L. Houlden will be our final illustration of this line of thinking. In his analysis of Eph. 5.22 he notes that the author constructs a parallel between the social conventions of his time and the eternal hierarchy of God-Christ-church. He suggests that the author of Ephesians understands both the wife's subordination and the eternal hierarchy as permanent dispositions of God:

> It is apparent to us that he over-estimated the permanence of the conventions of marriage as he knew them, and in this respect was carried away by the beauty of his scheme.[30]

Even so, Houlden would grant that the association of Christ and the church with the husband and wife gives the teaching about marriage a new "profundity." He writes, "The union of man and woman in marriage receives 'cosmic' roots; it is as deep and indestructable as Christ's God-given union with his people."[31]

In effect, all three exegetes understand the wife's subordination negatively — (1) as a regression away from equality between men and women (so Scroggs); (2) as a statement about the inferiority of women (so Fiorenza); and (3) as a social convention not at all relevant to

---

[28] Ibid., p. 269.
[29] Ibid., p. 270.
[30] See *Paul's Letters from Prison: Philippians, Colossians, Philemon, and Ephesians*, WPC (Philadelphia: Westminster [1970], 1977), p. 332.
[31] Ibid., p. 332.

twentieth century social reality (so Houlden). According to this way of
thinking, Ephesians or at least Eph. 5.22-24 stands *with* its culture,
mirroring and reinforcing patriarchal values.

This deceptively simple text receives positive interpretations from
other quarters. A second group of scholars agrees that Ephesians is a
product of its own culture. But their common tendency, differences not
withstanding, is to interpret the injunction for subordination as a
theological challenge to first century Mediterranean culture. That is, the
scholars below see Eph. 5.22-24 as standing *against* its culture.

The Swiss exegete M. Barth does not interpret the injunction for
subordination as something which makes the wife a servile, "bootlick-
ing" (in Barth's language) and dehumanized creature. He notes that
when Paul discusses the subordination of Christ, members of the church,
prophets, wives and the obedience of children and slaves, he uses the
middle or passive indicatives, participles or imperatives of the verbs "to
subordinate" and "to obey."[32] In his view, the use of the middle and
passive voices suggests the voluntary action of someone "giving in,
cooperating, assuming responsibility, and carrying a burden."[33] Applied
to Eph. 5.22-24 this means that the wife's subordination is first and
foremost an action freely accepted.

Barth would partially agree with Fiorenza — the wife's subordination is directed to a husband who must love her.[34] He writes, "The
subordination of the wife is now characterized as her response to the
husband's love." He differs from her by insisting that the presence of
Christ-like love lifts subordination away from patriarchal enslavement
and places it in a Christian way of life which brings unity,[35] love and joy
between husband and wife.[36] This metamorphosis of subordination
means that the wife's subordination does not lessen her dignity as a
person. Barth writes, "Jesus Christ demonstrates rather than loses his
dignity by his subordination to the Father."[37]

The connection between Christ and the wife is promising but
not self-evident. Barth does not indicate how this connection can be
made. Granted that at 1 Cor. 15.28b the verb ὑποταγίσεται is in the
middle voice, at Eph. 5.22 there is no verb at all! One would first have to
resolve the ellipsis of the verb and then argue that any verb understood
there ought to be in the middle voice. In addition, he does not notice that

---

[32] See *Ephesians*, p. 710, esp. n. 390 for examples.
[33] Ibid., p. 710.
[34] Ibid., p. 713.
[35] Ibid.
[36] Ibid., p. 710. Here Barth interprets 5.22 in light of 4.1-3.
[37] Ibid., p. 714. He lists 1 Cor. 15.28 and refers the reader to Phil. 2.6; Rom. 5.19;
8.3; John 1.14.

the church's subordination (cf. 5.21, 24a) is the primary paradigm for the wife's subordination, not that of Christ. Finally, how does he arrive at the issue of dignity? The context of 1 Cor. 15.20-28 addresses those last steps in the salvation process which unite all things to God. If there is a link between the subordination of Christ and that of the wife, in all likelihood it has to do with soteriology. If this is the case, then certainly the issue of dignity is relevant. I shall return to these points in the chapters which follow.

At this point we note that, according to Barth's interpretation, the injunction that wives be subordinate to their husbands challenges patriarchal values on two fronts. First, it presupposes the free choice of the wife — she acts as a free, willing and therefore morally responsible agent. Such an injunction is neither widespread nor commonplace in Greek literature dealing with marriage.[38] Second, her subordination to the husband's Christ-like love signals her connection to Christ in two ways: (1) through the husband's love and (2) through her subordination, which (somehow) manifests a dignity which parallels Christ's subordination to the Father.

The work of J. Cambier represents an approach similar to that of Barth. He also focuses on the verb "to subordinate." He notes that when the verb occurs in the Pauline Corpus, it indicates that the subordination demanded is to God's intent and order in the new creation, either negatively or positively.[39] According to Cambier, the doctrine of God's "order" for marriage is first expressed at Gen. 1-2, completed by Paul at 1 Cor. 3.23 and 11.3, and developed at Eph. 5.22-24.[40] It is within such a theological frame of reference that Cambier interprets the subordination of the wife. For him, the wife's subordination to the loving husband is a direct consequence of knowing God's will.

He supports this thesis by arguing that the injunction to the wife is formally attached to the preceding context, which begins at 5.17 ("Therefore, do not be foolish but understand what the *will of the Lord is*.") Since 5.21 is formally attached to 5.17 and also supplies the verb for 5.22, the demand that the whole community (5.21) and that the wife (5.22) be subordinate is interpreted as a direct result of knowing God's

---

[38] Here Barth (Ibid., pp. 708-709, n. 382) follows the work of Rengstorf ("Die neutestamentlichen Mahnungen an die Frau, sich dem Manne unterzuordnen," *Verbum Dei manet in aeternum. Festschrift für O. Schmitz* [Witten: Luther Verlag, 1953], pp. 131-145) who traces the use of ὑποτάσσω only to Plutarch's *Moralia* 142E and to Ps. Callisthenes' *Hist. Alexandri Magni* I 22.

[39] "Le grand mystère concernant le Christ et son Église," *Bib* 47 (1966):43-90, esp. p. 68.

[40] Ibid., pp. 64-65.

will and intent in the new creation as expressed at 5.17.[41] Cambier understands the injunction for subordination as standing *against* its culture because, as a loving response to the husband's Christ-like love, the wife's subordination manifests God's will and intent for the adoptive "sons of God" who form part of the new creation. Without the agapic element, the injunction would simply reflect the pagan practices of the day.[42]

Fiorenza, Barth and Cambier provide similar argumentation about the meaning of ὑποτάσσω, but with striking differences. They all establish the meaning of the verb without reference to the husband's injunction to love. Fiorenza interprets the verb in light of the dominant patriarchal culture, which leads to the conclusion that the wife's subordination is degrading. Barth and Cambier analyze the verb throughout the Pauline Corpus and connect it either to the dignity which believers and Christ exercise in relation to God (Barth) or, to the question of God's intent for the new creation (Cambier). I am inclined to think that the work of the last two scholars suggests that there may be a Pauline basis for a radical challenge to patriarchal subordination.

The suggestion that subordination is part of God's intent in the new creation is rather interesting. That the wife's subordination is linked to 5.17 suggests that such an interpretation is possible. However, Cambier's argument is not without its problems. Abbott (with others) argues that connections between 5.22 and 5.17-21 are purely formal.[43] If subordination is to be linked to the new creation, it cannot be based solely on connections between 5.22 and 5.17-21.

The interpretations of Fiorenza (i.e., the agapic and christological transformation of the address to husbands at Eph. 5.25), Barth (i.e., the "christological" dignity implied in the wife's subordination to the husband), and Cambier (i.e., subordination is connected to God's intent for the new creation) suggest that the author of Ephesians expands and therefore interprets the household code with a particular theological agenda in mind. That is, he is not simply exercising literary creativity as an end in itself but appears to be guided by three dominant concerns.

The first and most obvious concern is that the author wishes to alter what subordination means at Eph. 5.22, 24. The absence of the verb at Eph. 5.22 and 24b and its application to the church at v.24a — making the church the paradigm for the wife's subordination — makes this quite

---

[41] Ibid., pp. 57-58; see esp. pp. 68-69 for a summary of this point.

[42] Ibid., p. 69.

[43] *Ephesians*, p. 164. See BARTH, *Ephesians*, p. 608, n. 5 for a list of those who agree with Abbott and for those who argue that connections between 5.22 and 5.17-21 are more than formal.

clear. The nuance of the text cautions the reader not to interpret it at face value — it is not just a straightforward demand for the wife's subordination. Second, by linking that demand to christological, soteriological and ecclesiological elements, the suggestion that subordination is being radically reinterpreted by linking that demand to christological, soteriological and ecclesiological elements, and, the suggestion that subordination is being radically reinterpreted by means of some *theological agenda* not yet obvious find further support. That is, the author appears to have placed the injunction for subordination within a definite theological frame of reference. Third, the connection between Eph. 5.22 and 5.17, although not conclusive, may very well represent initial evidence of what may be part of the author's theological agenda. Because of the tenuous nature of the connection between 5.22 and 5.17, any argument which seeks to link the subordination of the wife *directly* to a specific theological agenda (i.e., God's intent for marriage in the new creation) would be best served if evidence can be drawn *directly* from the text itself.

Let me conclude this part of the discussion by stating that the question of whether Ephesians stands *with* or *against* its own culture will not be the primary focus of this study. Such a question can be answered only by means of accurate reconstructions of this or that first century Mediterranean social context. New Testament scholarship on this question is still in its infancy.[44] The questions I bring to the text are theological and literary: what, if any, *theological ideas* guided the author's use of *Pauline language* at Eph. 5.22-24? In other words, I am interested in tracing points of contact between Ephesians and the Pauline Corpus as these impinge upon the task of discovering the theological agenda guiding the construction of Eph. 5.22-24.

B. Thesis Statement

It is my contention that the theological agenda guiding the expansion of the injunction for subordination (5.22, 24) and the language used to justify it (5.23) are ultimately rooted in Pauline and Jewish theological reflections about Adam's role in the redemptive process. For lack of a better term, I call this kind of reflection Adam speculation. In what follows I shall argue that the author of Ephesians deleted the verb at 5.22 and 24b, placed the verb ὑποτάσσω ("subordination") at v. 24 and expanded the address to wives with the "head/body" (v.23) and "savior" language because he wanted to link Christian marriage to the New Adam and Eve relationship expressed at Eph. 5.31-32.

---

[44] E.g., see B.J. MALINA, review of *The First Urban Christians: The Social World of the Apostle Paul*, by W.A. MEEKS, in *JBL* 104 (1985):346-347.

My argument entails a twofold procedure. First, it will be necessary to demonstrate that the "subordination," "head/body" and "savior" language can be linked to either Pauline or Jewish forms of Adam speculation. If I can demonstrate this, then we shall have linguistic evidence *directy* from the text of Eph. 5.22-24 indicating that the rationale guiding the expansion of the address to wives is inextricably bound with Pauline New Creation theology. Second, it will then be necessary to demonstrate precisely how, in light of the first step, Eph. 5.22-24 can be linked the text of Eph. 5.31-32. The following survey will target the precise *cruces interpretum* involved in this study.

C. Eph. 5.22-24 and 5.31-32

At Eph. 5.31-32[45] we read

[31] ἀντὶ τούτου καταλείψει ἄνθρωπος [τὸν] πατέρα καὶ [τὴν] μητέρα καὶ προσκολληθήσεται πρὸς τὴν γυναῖκα αὐτοῦ, καὶ ἔσονται οἱ δύο εἰς σάρκα μίαν. [32] τὸ μυστήριον τοῦτο μέγα ἐστίν· ἐγὼ δὲ λέγω εἰς Χριστὸν καὶ εἰς τὴν ἐκκλησίαν.[46].

The question is, did Gen. 2.24 influence the expansion of the address to wives and husbands (Eph. 5.22-30)? If so, then we shall have significant evidence to suggest that the theological agenda guiding the expansion of Eph. 5.22-24 may be rooted in Pauline new creation

---

[45] The problems connected with the interpretation of Eph. 5.31-32 deserve the attention of a separate monograph. Therefore I can only indicate, in brief fashion, two of the critical issues. (1) What is the precise meaning of the term μυστήριον ("mystery")? The majority of scholars tend to define the term as something once hidden but now revealed (by God) to believers in Christ. For the purposes of this study the above interpretation of μυστήριον will be accepted. The debate is not closed. See R. BROWN, *The Semitic Background of the Term "Mystery" in the New Testament*, Facet Books, Biblical Series 21 (Philadelphia: Fortress Press, 1968) and more recently, Chrys C. Caragounis, *The Ephesian Mysterion: Meaning and Content* (Lund: CWK Gleerup, 1977). (2) Does the μυστήριον refer simply to the creation of Adam and Eve in the context of Gen. 2.24, to the Christ/church relationship in the context of Eph. 5.22-33 in light of the text from Gen. 2.24 (i.e. the allegorical reading of the text by the church fathers, see H. SCHLIER, V. WARNACH, *Die Kirche im Epheserbrief* [Münster: Aschendorff, 1949], pp. 70-71, n. 99; Bornkamm, *TDNT* IV, p. 823), to the Christ/church and husband/wife relationship, as most Catholic scholars would argue (see Brown, Ibid., p. 65), or to some other possibility (e.g. Cambier ["Le grand mystère concernant le Christ et son Église," pp. 43-90] argues that the mystery only refers to Christ and the church, see esp. pp. 44-45).

[46] The RSV reads, "[31] For this reason a man sall leave his father and mother and be joined to his wife, and the two shall become one flesh. [32] This mystery is a profound one, and I am saying that it refers to Christ and the church."

theology.[47] This evidence, in turn, could lead to uncovering how, if at all, the injunction for subordination challenges the "valuations" of patriarchal domination in marriage.

The majority of scholars who raise the question agree that the literary impact of Gen. 2.24 can be discerned only in the address to husbands. It does not extend to the address to wives (Eph. 5.22-24).[48] The argument often advanced is that the presence of σώματα ("bodies") at v.28, σάρκα ("flesh") at v. 29 and σώματος ("body") at v.30 can be explained in part by appealing to the presence of the σάρκα μίαν ("one flesh") imagery at 5.31.[49] In this instance, the text from Genesis is thought to influence the address to husbands, at least from v.28 onwards. Therefore, the text of Gen. 2.24 is relevant to marriage because it influenced the terms and images found in the second half of the injunction to husbands. The injunction for subordination (5.22-24) is usually not perceived as related to the text of Gen. 2.24 (Eph. 5.31).

L. Ramaroson and J. Paul Sampley are exceptions to the rule. Ramaroson reasons that at Eph. 5.23c the phrase αὐτὸς σωτὴρ τοῦ σώματος ("he, savior of the body") seems out of place. Reference to the husband (5.23a) appears to be primarily concerned with the question of his authority. The phrase is out of place because it does not refer primarily to authority but to love "puisque c'est proprement l'amour qui pousse à sauver." It is odd that the injunction for subordination contains a statement about love when it appears to be interested in establishing the husband's authority.[50] According to Ramaroson, saving love has little to do with the authority of the husband. Yet, he continues, because 5.23c signals Christ's saving love, it actually prepares the reader for the injunction to love at 5.25. The injunction to love, in turn, prepares the reader for a remote verse, Eph. 5.31 (Gen. 2.24), where Christ and the church are described as "one flesh," an image which traditionally describes married love.[51]

---

[47] The proposal holds true only if Christ and the church are understood as the New Adam and Eve at Eph. 5.31-32. For differing reasons, most scholars hold this to be the case, as I point out below.

[48] E.g., R. SCHNACKENBURG (*Der Brief an die Epheser* EKKNT 10 (Zürich/Einsiedeln/Köln: Benzinger, 1982], p. 259-262) suggests that the "one flesh" unity articulated at Gen. 2.24 reinforces the exhortation that the husband ought to love his wife as his own "flesh". The injunction for subordination does not enter the discussion. See also Brown, Ibid.

[49] For a recent statement of the position see A.T. LINCOLN, "The use of the OT in Ephesians [Gen. 2.24; Ex. 20.12; Is. 57.19 & Ps. 68.18]," *JSNT* 14 (1982):16-57. See also Sampley, *One Flesh*, pp. 84-85, 113-114; SCHNACKENBURG, *Der Brief*, p. 261, and n. 665.

[50] L. RAMAROSON, "'L'Église, corps du Christ' dans les écrits pauliniens: simples esquisses," *ScEs* 30 (1978):129-141, see p. 139.

[51] Ibid., pp. 138-139.

No doubt the themes of saving love and marriage are related, but the approach he takes is weak for a number of reasons. First, Ramaroson does not show how the injunction for subordination or how the husband's headship (i.e., the husband's authority, as he sees it) relates to Eph. 5.31-32. That is, even if we grant him his argument — 5.23c does ultimately relate to 5.31 — can the same be said about the wife's subordination and the husband's headship? He is silent on these questions. Second, his argument that Christ's role as savior suggests love, prepares for 5.25 and ultimately for 5.31, presupposes the integration of several themes based on a theological method appropriate to cannonical criticism or systematic theology.

Sampley argues that the "one flesh" imagery at Gen. 2.24 (Eph. 5.31) and the κεφαλή (5.23: "head"), σῶμα (v.23c, v.28, v.30: "body") and μέλη (v.30: "members") terminology are "naturally" associated with one another.[52] The presence of the "one flesh" imagery at Eph. 5.31 permits the introduction of the head/body imagery at 5.22-24.[53] Sampley advances a second argument. Following the work of others, he argues that texts such as 1 Cor. 11.8, 9 and 1 Tim. 2.11-14 and 1 Pet. 3.5, 6 "all contain the verb ὑποτάσσομαι and ground the subordination in the Torah."[54] Since Eph. 5.22-33 contains both the verb ὑποτάσσομαι (5.24a) and a text from Torah (i.e., Gen. 2.24 cited at Eph. 5.31), the whole of Eph. 5.22-23 was constructed with 5.31 in mind; the citation from Gen. 2.24 undergirds the address to both wives and husbands.

Sampley's position has merit. First, his arguments are based on the language of the text itself. Second, his treatment of the question is disciplined; it seldom ventures beyond the levels of literary analysis. However, his position has not gone unchallenged.

In a recent article, A.T. Lincoln focuses on the "Achilles heel" of Sampley's position. Lincoln agrees that the literary pattern associating ὑποτάσσω with a text from Torah does exist within Pauline literature. But he rejects the contention that Eph. 5.22-33 fits this literary pattern because in the final analysis "subordination is not in view in this particular verse" (i.e., Eph. 5.31 [Gen. 2.24]). According to Lincoln, the point of Eph. 5.31 is the *mutual* "one flesh" relationship and not subordination.[55] The argument is that Eph. 5.31 has little to do with the subordination of the wife since the question of *mutuality* conflicts with the idea of *subordination*.

---

[52] See *One Flesh*, p. 84.
[53] Ibid., pp. 113-114. In addition, Sampley proposes that the presence of σάρξ at 5.29b indicates "clear internal evidence that Gen. 2.24 (Eph. 5.31) is informing the author's expansion of the Haustafel address to husbands," see *One Flesh*, p. 143.
[54] Ibid., p. 97.
[55] "The use of the OT in Ephesians," p. 36.

Lincoln's criticism brings us to the heart of the problem. The question is, does the injunction for subordination relate to the mutual "one flesh" relationship depicted at 5.31? Sampley's arguments based on the analysis of vocabulary and literary patterns cannot answer the objections raised by Lincoln. My solution is that we must take into account *the theological nature of the language* found at 5.22-24. No one has attempted to relate the injunction for subordination (Eph. 5.22-24) to the mutual "one flesh" relationship of 5.31-32 based on the nature of the language found at 5.22-24.

In the chapters which follow I will argue that both the injunction for subordination and the language used to justify it are rooted in Pauline and Jewish forms of Adam speculation and therefore, that the construction and interpretation of 5.22-24 is best understood in light of Eph. 5.31-32. Ultimately I shall have to make clear precisely how the subordination demanded of the wife at 5.22-24 can be linked to the mutual "one flesh" of Christ and the church at 5.31-32.

The problem of connecting the injunction for subordination at 5.22-24 with the quotation from Gen. 2.24 at 5.31 raises an ancillary question, one which has been seriously underestimated in previous studies. Why is the text of Gen. 2.24 applied *only* to the Christ/church relationship? Stated negatively, why is the text of Gen. 2.24 not applied to the husband/wife relationship? That we find a text which traditionally relates to marriage (i.e., Gen. 2.24) in a passage which by literary design (i.e., *Haustafel*) addresses marriage is not surprising.[56] That this text is quoted in such a passage and yet *not directly applied to husbands and wives is quite surprising!* Why is this the case?

Previous scholarship provides a two step process. Scholars first focus on the eschatological role of the Christ/church relationship of the New Adam and Eve. Some then apply this information in their analysis of the analogies at 5.22-24.

With regard to the eschatological nature of the Christ/church relationship, many take Christ and the church as the New Adam and Eve of the New Creation. They reason that the application of Gen. 2.24 to the Christ/church relationship at least implies that Christ and the church are to be understood as countertypes to Adam and Eve. H. Schlier argues this very point, proposing that the author of Ephesians applies Gen. 2.24 to Christ and the church to counter a Gnostic interpretation thought to have some currency during the last part of the first century

---

[56] In the following texts Gen. 2.24 is associated with human marriage in varying ways, cf. Mk. 10.7-9; Mt. 19.5; 1 Cor. 6.16.

A.D. But he does not discuss the subordination of the wife at all.[57]
Schnackenburg simply notes that the Christ/church relationship is similar
to that of Adam and Eve. Like Schlier, Schnackenburg does not
associate subordination with Eph. 5.31-32.[58] However, when he and
others consider the analogies, the conclusion is normally that Christian
marriage is now given an eschatological context[59] or is given cosmological roots.[60]

Examples like these could easily be multiplied. Ultimately scholars
account for the application of Gen. 2.24 to Christ and the church by
inferring that the application of a text which speaks about Adam and Eve
suggests the likelihood that Christ and the church are the New Adam and
Eve of the New Creation. Scholars never make precise how the "one
flesh" *mutuality* of Eph. 5.31-32 is linked to the wife's subordination,
especially if Christian marriage is given an eschatological or cosmological
context. Lincoln's criticisms of Sampley (and others) still stand.

My proposal is that since the wife/husband relationship does not
enjoy a fully realized eschatological existence, the text from Gen. 2.24 is
not *directly* applied to them. However, I would argue that the language
of subordination and of headship is the means by which the husband and
wife attain the "one flesh" mutual unity of the New Adam and Eve
relationship expressed at Eph. 5.31-32. Therefore, I would contend that
the exhortation for subordination and its justification represents the
author's understanding of how the husband and wife become "one flesh"
not as the first Adam and Eve *were "one flesh"* but as the New Adam
and Eve *are "one flesh."*

D. The Structure of This Study

The overall argument of this study is as follows. In the next chapter I
examine the logical structure of the injunction for subordination. I argue

---

[57] He writes, "Für den Apostel spricht das Zitat aus Gen. 2.24 nicht von dem
einzelnen Mann und seiner Frau und ihrer Ehe, sondern von dem Verhältnis Adams zu
Eva." See *Der Brief an die Epheser* (Düsseldorf: Patmos-Verlag, 1957), p. 262. Others
also note the Adam/Eve Christ/Church typology, see A.M. DUBARLE, "L'origine dans
l'Ancien Testament de la notion paulinienne de l'Église Corps du Christ," *Studiorum
Paulinorum Congressus Internationalis Catholicus*, AnBib 17-18 (Rome: Pontifical
Biblical Institute Press, 1962), vol. 17 pp. 231-240, esp. pp. 237-238; P. ANDRIESSEN, "La
nouvelle Ève, corps du nouvel Adam," in *Aux Origines de l'Église*, Recherches Bibliques
VII, J. GIBLET, et. al. (Louvain: Desclée de Brouwer, 1965), pp. 87-109.
[58] See *Der Brief*, pp. 259-260. Houlden (*Ephesians*, p. 335) notes that if reference to
Adam is intended at Eph. 5.31, it is not to the "inclusive" Adam of 1 Cor. 15.22, into
whom believers are incorporated. Rather, reference is now made to the marriage of
Christ to the Church, as of Adam to Eve. Examples of this interpretation are common.
[59] SCHNACKENBURG, *Der Brief*, p. 260.
[60] HOULDEN, *Ephesians*, p. 332.

that the logical structure of Eph. 5.22-24 indicates that the structural and theological core of the passage is the phrase "he, savior of the body" (5.23c). That is, I demonstrate that the injunction for subordination is carefully centered around a soteriological statement (5.23c) which in turn qualifies the christological statement at 5.23b ("just as Christ is head of the church"). In the third chapter I make clear that the soteriology of 5.23c is based on a type of Adam speculation which the author develops in his treatment of Christ's death at Eph. 2.14-18. Therefore the Adamic character of this text emerges from an examination of the language used to describe Christ's saving role. In the fourth chapter I demonstrate that the noun κεφαλή (Eph. 5.23: "head") and the verb ὑποτάσσω (Eph. 5.22, 24: "subordination")[61] have their origins in Pauline christological texts which focus on Adam/Christ typology. In the fifth chapter I interpret the injunction for subordination in light of the previous chapters. In the final chapter I demonstrate how the address to wives can be interpreted in light of Eph. 5.31-32.

---

[61] Actually, the verb does not appear at v. 22. In the next chapter I argue that the ellipsis of the verb at v.22 is best resolved by reading the participle from v.21 (i.e., ὑποτασσώμενοι) at v.22.

CHAPTER II

The Structure of 5.21-24: Subordination and Christology

A. Introduction

The contention that Eph. 5.22-24 contains language drawn from Pauline theological reflections about Adam must be supported by specific features of the text itself. Arguments focusing on the language of the text will follow this chapter. In the present chapter I focus on the surface structure of Eph. 5.22-24. I argue that the logical structure of vv.22-24 indicates that the "head/body" and "subordination" language cluster is ultimately dependent upon the soteriological statement about Christ at v.23c. We shall see that the author of Ephesians has revised the injunction for the wife's subordination with the goal of linking that injunction to soteriological (v.23c) and christological (v.23b) statements about Christ. The exegesis which follows makes clear that the author connects the wife to Christ by means of subordination (v.22), her relationship to her husband (v.23) and to the church (v.24). Thus the central role and importance of Christ as "head" and "savior" will provide the major clue for understanding that subordination cannot be properly understood outside of the christological and soteriological nature of the "head/body" language.

An examination of the logical structure of vv.22-24 should not be underestimated for two reasons. First, scholars normally avoid discussion of the structure.[1] When they do discuss the logical structure or the flow of thought, scholars disagree as to the precise focus of Eph. 5.22-33. This disagreement about focus is directly related to the disagreements about the structure or the text. Which relationship or level of the text should be understood as central, that of Christ and the church or the husband and the wife? Clearly the text addresses the wife and exhorts her to be subordinate. Yet, the Christ/church relationship and the husband also play a critical role. Barth provides a concise summary statement on the problem:

> Differing descriptions of the structure reveal whether the commentator attributes pre-eminence to the husband/wife topic or to the statements on Christ and the church. A decision between them need not be made. In this passage both topics are central, and both are ontologically and noetically

so closely tied together that they cannot be unstrung — not even for the reconstruction of an original supposedly Jewish or Greek *Haustafel*.[2]

Barth's criticism of other is quite correct; both levels of the passage are intimately connected and cannot be separated.

A few scholars are sensitive to this point. For example, Cambier connects the two levels of the text by postulating the existence of a doctrinal level — where the "deeper meaning" resides — which he applies to Christ and the church. The wife/husband relationship is then understood as representing the parenetic level of the passage. The connections between the two levels would then be based on the nuptial character of both levels of the passage itself.[3] Cambier's distinctions are useful from the prespective of dogmatic theology. They help distinguish between two levels of the text and this division conforms to the analogical nature of the text.

Sampley's literary approach yields insight into the structure based on the function of the analogies. He detects a pattern which alternates between the "earthly sphere" of Christ and the church (vv.23b-24a).[4] Like Cambier, Sampley refuses to make sharp distinctions between the Christ/church and wife/husband levels of the text.[5]. The comparative particles which pepper the text presuppose an essential interrelationship between the two levels of the text.[6] Yet he would argue that "it is not surprising in Ephesians to see the author's attention focused clearly on Christ and the church — even within the Haustafel form. In fact, it would almost seem in 5:21-33 that this concern has nearly eclipsed the Haustafel itself."[7]

Both Cambier and Sampley have the following in common. They agree that the analogies hold the key to interpreting the internal dynamics of the text. They agree that the theme of vv.22-24 is the wife's subordination. For differing reasons they consider the Christ/church relationship as dominant either theologically (Cambier) or comparatively (Sampley).

---

[1] Sampley (*One Flesh*, p. 103) is quite correct to point out that the issue of the logical structure of the text is normally avoided. Schlier does not treat the topic at all, cf. *Der Brief*, pp. 250-279, neither does C. Masson, *L'Épître de Saint Paul aux Éphésiens* (Paris/Neuchatel: Delachaux & Niestlé S.A., 1953), pp. 210-216. The one exception to this state of affairs is the recent commentary by Schnackenburg (*Der Brief*, pp. 248-264) whose *Analyse* (cf. pp. 248-249) and *Eklärung* (pp. 250-254) are quite sensitive to the logical flow of the text.

[2] See *Ephesians*, p. 659.

[3] Cambier, "Le grand mystère concernant le Christ et son Église," pp. 48, 59.

[4] See *One Flesh*, pp. 103-108 for his analysis of vv.22-23 as a whole.

[5] Ibid., p. 103.

[6] Ibid., p. 107.

[7] Ibid., p. 106.

Although I am in basic agreement with the general orientation outlined above, I think that the basic structure of vv.22-24 is still misunderstood because the connections between soteriology, Christology and the wife's subordination have not been addressed. My suggestion is that we think of the Christ/church relationship as being analogically prior to the wife/husband relationship. In this way we can agree on the importance of the Christ/church relationship without underestimating the central theme of the passage: subordination.

B. The Logical Structure of 5.22-24

Eph. 5.22-24

21 ὑποτασσόμενοι ἀλλήλοις ἐν φόβῳ Χριστοῦ

22	αἱ γυναῖκες τοῖς ἰδίοις ἀνδράσιν ὡς τῷ κυρίῳ
23a	ὅτι ἀνήρ ἐστιν κεφαλὴ τῆς γυναικὸς
b	ὡς καὶ ὁ Χριστὸς κεφαλὴ τῆς ἐκκλησίας,
c	αὐτὸς σωτὴρ τοῦ σώματος
24a	ἀλλὰ ὡς ἡ ἐκκλησία ὑποτάσσεται τῷ Χριστῷ
b	οὕτως καὶ αἱ γυναῖκες τοῖς ἀνδράσιν ἐν παντί.

What follows is a verse by verse analysis of the salient features in vv.22-24. The intent is to isolate the logical structure of the passage which in turn will highlight the connection between christology and subordination.

1. Eph. 5.22: αἱ γυναῖκες τοῖς ἰδίοις ἀνδράσιν ὡς τῷ κυρίῳ

It is interesting to note the ellipsis of the verb in v.22.[8] An ellipsis is neither unusual nor uncommon in texts of antiquity. But what is striking about this particular ancient verse is that the author addresses the question of the wife's subordination without using any form of the verb "to subordinate"! How should the ellipsis be interpreted? Two options present themselves.

On the one hand, the major verbal idea from the previous linguistic unit could supply the major verbal idea as a resolution of the ellipsis. In this case, the participle of v.21 (ὑποτασσόμενοι) can be read at v.22, thus supplying the latter verse with a verbal idea. On the other hand, some form of the copula (i.e., the verb "to be") could be assumed or understood at v.22 and thus supply the major verbal idea. Either option would reflect a common practice in antiquity.

Most commentators usually assume that the participle of v.21 should be read at v.22 as a resolution of the ellipsis of the verb. As a matter of

---

[8] That is, the absence of any verb or verb form within the Greek sentence.

course, they do not consider the option of simply reading in some form of the copula here, and for good reason. The manuscript evidence, the context of vv.22-24 and the parallels to the text do not support this position.

Manuscript evidence does not support this way of resolving the ellipsis. Most agree that the better manuscripts indicate an ellipsis of the verb at 5.22.[9] In addition, manuscripts which do contain verbs at v.22 typically avoid any insertion of the copula. They normally read some form of the verb ὑποτάσσω either as an imperative (cf. mss D F G, etc.) or something else (cf. mss A I P etc.).[10] Although the manuscript evidence for reading the participle from v.21 at v.22 is cogent, scholars pay little if any attention to stylistic and internal considerations in support of the present consensus. What follows are my own contributions towards this end.

Structural as well as grammatical parallels between vv.21, 22, and vv.22a, 24b suggest that the participle in v.21 — and not some form of the copula — should be read at v.22 in the middle voice with an imperatival force.[11]

In v.21 the phrase which follows the participle is in the dative plural as is the object of the unspecified verb at v.22 (i.e., the ellipsis). The parallel construction of plural subjects as well as dative plurals at vv.21 and 22 suggests that the same verbal idea at v.21 could be read at v.22. A second consideration confirms this. In both vv.22a and 24b there exists an ellipsis of the verb followed by a construction in the dative plural. The ellipsis of v.24b is best resolved by a reading in the verb from v.24a. By doing this, the general topic of 5.22-24 — the subordination of the wife — is reiterated. Because v.24b parallels v.24a grammatically and in terms of vocabulary it seems reasonable to suggest that the participle of v.24a should supply the verbal idea for v.24b. The context of vv.21-24 — the subordination of the wife — also supports the suggestion that the

---

[9] Some go a step further and suggest that the ellipsis be resolved with an imperative verbal idea. Cf. ABBOTT, *Ephesians*, p. 166; BARTH, *Ephesians*, p. 610, n. 8 (who amplifies Abbott's position); MASSON, *L'Épître*, p. 210; See SCHNACKENBURG, *Der Brief*, p. 251 for a discussion of the manuscript evidence. See p.252 where he asserts that the ellipsis at v.22 must be "filled in" with an imperative. However, he offers no arguments to support his claim.

[10] Aside from the scholars already mentioned, see also the manuscript evidence listed in NESTLE-ALAND, *Novum Testamentum Graece*, 26th Edition (Stuttgart: Deutsche Bibelgesellschaft, 1979), p. 512.

[11] Concerning the imperatival function of the participle see N. TURNER, *A Grammer of New Testament Greek*, vol. III (Edinburgh: T. & T. Clark, 1963), p. 343 and n. 1 for bibliography. On whether the function of "imperatival participle" stems from Semitic or Hellenistic linguistic influences see P. KANJUPARAMBIL, "Imperative Participles in Rom 12:9-21," *JBL* 102 (1983):285-288.

verb "to subordinate" be understood at v.24b and v.22 since that is precisely the issue being developed.[12]

That this verbal idea be interpreted with an imperatival force is clear from the following. First, one can detect a consistent stylistic pattern concerning the address to each of the household members. The plural or generic vocative is used with imperatives at Eph. 5.25 (husbands); 6.1 (children); 6.4 (fathers); 6.5 (slaves); 6.9 (masters). The address to the wives, in the plural vocative, fits this pattern if we read the participle of v.21 in v.22 with an imperatival force. In light of the stylistic pattern of 5.21-6.9 as a whole, it is reasonable to suggest that at v.22 we should read the participle from v.21, and with an imperatival force.

Second, the imperatival form of the participle in v.21 occurs in Col. 3,18, the closest literary parallel to Eph. 5.22. The parallels between Col. 3.18 and Eph. 5.22 support the suggestion that at Eph. 5.22 an imperatival thrust in the verbal idea would not be out of place.[13] In light of the above considerations (i.e., the grammar and context of Eph. 5.22 as well as the strong parallels between Eph. 5.22 and Col. 3.18), it seems clear that the participle of v.21 should supply the main verbal idea for v.22, with an imperatival force.

That the verbal idea should be a middle imperative as opposed to an active imperative is confirmed by the following analysis. Whenever ὑποτάσσω occurs in the active voice within the Pauline Corpus (be it in the form of a verb, participle or infinitive), it suggests the idea that coercive force or power is being used[14] or that some kind of control over something else is to be understood.[15]

However, when it occurs in either the middle or passive voice (regardless of its verbal form), it suggests the idea of cooperation, the act of a free agent.[16] Since the ellipsis of the verb in Eph. 5.22 and 24b is to be supplied from vv.21 and 24 respectively — where the participle (v.21)

---

[12] In addition, it is because both vv.22 and 24b have the same articular feminine plural subjects (v.22 in the vocative; v.24b in the nominative), an ellipsis of the verb and dative plurals as well as qualifying phrases in the dative plural that I am convinced that the ellipsis of the verb in v.22 should be resolved by means of reading in the verbal idea from the previous linguistic unit (as is the case with v.24b). Concerning the syntactical overlap between the articular vocative and nominative cases see A.T. ROBINSON, *A Grammar of the Greek New Testament in Light of Historical Research* (Nashville: Broodmans Press, 1934), p. 757; H.E. DANA, and J.R. MANTEY, *A Manual of the Greek New Testament* (New York: The McMillan Co., 1944), p. 144. See J. GNILKA, *Der Epheserbrief*, HTKNT 10.2 (Freiburg: Herdes, 1971), p. 272 for cogent arguments concerning the presence of the vocative at v.22.

[13] I treat the parallels between Eph. 5.22 and Col. 3.18 in note 31 below.

[14] Cf. Rom. 8.7, 20; Phil. 3.21; 1 Cor. 15.27 [3 times], 28a.

[15] Rom. 14.32.

[16] Cf. Eph. 5.21, 24 and 1 Cor. 14.34; 15.28a; 16.16; Rom. 13.1, 5; Col. 3.18; Tit. 2.9; 3.1.

and the verb (v.24a) are in the middle voice — it is reasonable to argue that the imperative at v.22 should be in the middle voice.

Finally, in Col. 3.18, the source for Eph. 5.22, ὑποτάσσω occurs in the second person plural, middle imperative. The fact that this verb appears in this form here and elsewhere within the Pauline Corpus further confirms the argument that at Eph. 5.22 the imperatival verbal idea should be interpreted in the middle/passive voice.[17]

In light of the above analysis of the ellipsis in v.22, the following observation seems warranted. The ellipsis of the verb functions to alert the reader that the verb ὑποτάσσω is not to be taken simply at face value. In support of this contention, let me point out precisely how the ellipsis of the verb in v.22 can affect the reader's understanding of the injunction for subordination in terms of the logical relationships between v.22 and what comes before it.

We now can admit that v.22 is grammatically dependent on v.21. That is, v.21 supplies the main verbal idea for v.22. However, formal considerations lead us to note that the articular vocative plural of v.22 introduces a new subject. That is, v. 22 must be understood as materially independent of v.21. The point here is that the author is able to introduce an entirely new subject (i.e., the *Haustafel*, which formally begins v.22 and ends with 6.9) while simultaneously linking it to the previous context.

Let me illustrate the point grammatically. The participle at v.21 is the last of five consecutive participles, which are dependent on the second person plural imperative πληροῦσθε ("be filled") at 5.18. Thus from a grammatical point of view, it is reasonable to suggest that the exhortation to "be filled with the Spirit" at v.18 is followed by what we might call concrete examples of how one becomes "filled with the Spirit." The participle at v.21 (ὑποτασσόμενοι) is the last of five participial illustrations of what the author understands as being "filled with the Spirit" (5.18).

The author has connected not only the act of mutual subordination (v.21: "be subordinate to one another") to the "life in the Spirit" (v.18), he has also twice associated the act of subordination with Christology v.21: "in the fear of Christ"; v.22: "as to the Lord"). Thus the grammar (the ellipsis of the verb) and the immediate context of v.22 (the syntactical connection between 5.18 and 22) function to alert the reader that the author is giving a particular nuance to the injunction for subordination. My own speculation is that he wishes to link the lifestyle of the household with a life of being filled with the Spirit.[18]

---

[17] See 1 Cor. 16.16; Tit. 2.9: 3.1. See BARTH, *Ephesians*, p. 710, n. 390 for bibliography on the function of ὑποτάσσω in the active and middle/passive voices.

[18] Against ABBOTT, (*Ephesians*, p. 164), who holds that connections between vv.18

To summarize, the ellipsis of the verb is our first clue that the injunction for the wife's subordination is connected with Christology. The ellipsis is best resolved by reading the participle from v.21 at v.22 as a middle imperative. Structurally, the injunction for subordination is connected to the author's treatment of life in the spirit. Thus the injunction for subordination is twice connected to Christology at v.21 and v.22.

We have been alerted — in a minimal way — to the author's christocentric interests by means of the analysis of the grammatical and contextual features of v.22 (i.e., the ellipsis, the syntactical links between 5.18 and 22). Treatment can now be given to a second critical feature of v.22: the phrase "as to the Lord." An analysis of this phrase will confirm that the injunction for subordination is logically dependent on the wife's relationships with the Lord.

In verse 22 wives are commanded to be "subordinate" to their husbands *"as to the Lord."* The concern of v.22 is to link the wife/husband relationship to her relationship with the Lord. This association of the two relationships indicates a bi-dimensional quality of the wife's relational existence, the horizontal (wife/husband) and vertical (wife/Christ) dimensions. The wife's subordination to the husband is ultimately directed to the Lord, as is the case with the church (v.24).

It has long been noted that the phrase "as to the Lord" controls the interpretation of v.22. I agree with this position but would suggest that a careful examination of this phrase in relation to what follows it reveals that in fact it is essential for the argument developed within the address to the wives. The question is precisely how v.22 is related to what follows it.[19]

A number of commentators resolve this question on grammatical grounds: the ὅτι clause links v.22 to v.23. This grammatical observations is rather obvious; what is not so obvious is the conceptual link between v.22 and what follows it. That is, what is the movement of thought from v.22 to v.23? Various approaches are taken to address this conceptual question. Some focus on the rhetorical features of 5.22-24;[20] others argue

_____

and 22 are purely formal; others go beyond Abbott's interpretation, but do not see the connections between a life in the Spirit and subordination; see SAMPLEY, *One Flesh*, p. 116. I shall return to this association in chapter 5 below.

[19] The following note the critical function of the phrase "as to the Lord." They are not unanimous as to the precise importance of the phrase. See BARTH, *Ephesians*, pp. 611-613; ABBOTT, *Ephesians*, p. 166; CAMBIER, "Le grand mystère concernant le Christ et son Église," pp. 63-64; SAMPLEY, *One Flesh*, pp. 121-122; SCHLIER, *Der Brief*, p. 253; GNILKA, *Epheserbrief*, pp. 275-276.

[20] SAMPLEY, *One Flesh*, p. 122.

that vv.23-24 substantiate or justify the injunction given at v.22;[21] others suggest that vv.23-24 "clarify" v.22.[22]

Promising insights have come from scholars such as Schlier and Gnilka. For example, Schlier argues that the phrase "as to the Lord" establishes a foundation for the analogy in v.23 (he does not include v.24).[23] Gnilka advances the discussion with the suggestion that the phrase prepares for the Christ/church analogies in vv.23-24 as a whole[24] Unfortunately, neither one offers arguments in support of their positions. There is need to understand the conceptual link between v.22 and v.23 if the structure of vv.22-24 is to be clearly seen and if we are to understand how that structure impinges on the injunction for subordination.

A comparison of Eph. 5.22 with relevant parallels will help answer the question. The phrase "as to the Lord" (Eph. 5.22) does not occur in the address to wives at Col. 3.18, its closest literary parallel. Nor does the phrase occur within other *Haustafeln* texts of the New Testament in the address to wives.[25] Rather, it occurs at Eph. 6.7 and Col. 3.23 in connection with slaves.

In all three instances the phrase appears to be part of a formula whereby a vertical dimension (i.e., person to Christ) is being integrated into an horizontal dimension (i.e., person to person).[26] For example, the emphasis in Eph. 6.7 and Col. 3.23 underscores the importance of understanding that the master/slave relationship must be viewed not from an anthropocentric but from a christocentric perspective. The same sort of emphasis seems to be present in v.22. The wife/husband relationship is first addressed, then it is qualified by the heavenly wife/Lord relationship with the phrase "as to the Lord."[27]

It is peculiar that the author of Ephesians would address the wife

---

[21] MASSON, *L'Epître*, p. 211; SCHNACKENBURG, *Der Brief*, p. 252.

[22] BARTH, *Ephesians*, pp. 612-613.

[23] *Der Brief*, p. 253.

[24] *Epheserbrief*, pp. 275-276.

[25] For example, cf. Col. 3.18-4.1; 1 Pet. 3.1-7; 1 Tim. 2.9-15 and Tit. 3.1-6.

[26] Few exegetes point out the bi-dimensional aspect of Eph. 5.22. Perhaps the importance of Col. 3.18 (the address to wives) has been overestimated at the expense of Col. 3.23 and Eph. 6.7 (the address to slaves). Although exegetes take these last two texts into consideration, they nonetheless do not perceive their potential for interpreting Eph. 5.22. See SCHLIER, *Der Brief*, p. 253; ABBOTT, *Ephesians*, p. 165; GNILKA, *Epheserbrief*, p. 275; SAMPLEY, *One Flesh*, pp. 122-123; CAMBIER, "Le grand mystère concernant le Christ et son Église," pp. 60-63.

[27] It seems reasonable to suggest that the author of Ephesians had access to the phrase "as to the Lord" perhaps from Eph. 6.7, or, Col. 3.23 or to similar sources behind these texts. That Eph. 5.22 represents an edited version of Col. 3.18 *alone* is probably not the case. For a treatment of both this question and the extensive parallels between Eph. 5.22 and Col. 3.18 see note 31 below.

with part of a phrase that, aside from its presence in 5.22, is restricted to the address to slaves. Why did he not use the phrase found in the address to wives in Col. 3.18 ("as in fitting in the Lord") or even the phrase from Eph. 6.5 ("as to Christ") to initiate his address to the wives? The use of either phrase would certainly have avoided the possibility of coloring the wife/husband relationship with undesirable connotation imported with the phrase "as to the Lord."[28]

I submit that the author of Ephesians found the phrase "as to the Lord" a most suitable linguistic and conceptual vehicle precisely because it introduces a vertical or christocentric dimension (person to Lord) within what begins with the horizontal dimension (i.e., person to person).[29]

As with Eph. 6.7 and Col. 3.23, at Eph. 5.22 the phrase "as to the Lord" maintains the integrity of the horizontal relationship (wife to husband) while placing emphasis on the vertical relationship (wife to Lord).[30] Thus while the phrase "as to the Lord" helps emphasize the direction of the wife's act of subordination, in its present form at 5.22 (i.e., without the phrase "as to men"), it safeguards the integrity of the horizontal relationship.[31]

That is, in all three texts the individual is commanded (imperatives

---

[28] If Eph. 5.22 does represent a combination of Col. 3.18 (the articular vocative) Eph 6.7 and Col. 3.23 ("as to the Lord"), then the deletion of the phrase καὶ οὐκ ἀνθρώποις (Eph. 6.7; Col. 3.23) is understandable in that the presence of this phrase could lead to the interpretation that only the wife/Lord relationship is essential, at the expense of jeopardizing the integrity of the wife/husband relationship. Moreover, it would be difficult to argue that the wife is intimately related to the husband — as his "body," "self" or "flesh" (v.28) — with the presence of "and not to men" at 5.22.

[29] Against F.W. BEARE, "Epistle to the Ephesians," *Interpreters Bible*, G.A. Buttrick, ed. (Nashville: Abingdon Press, 1953), who argues that with the phrase "as to the Lord" the author of Ephesians carried too far the analogy between the Christ/church and husband/wife relationship.

[30] The advantage of interpreting 5.22 in light of 6.7 and/or Col. 3.23 (the address to slaves) is that both of these texts consistently emphasize the importance of directing the action "to the Lord." The author's interest in this directional focus manifests itself with the phrase "as to the Lord."

[31] To suggest that Eph. 5.22 is derived from Col. 3.18 is partially correct, especially in light of the grammatical parallels. In both instances ὡς ("as") is deictic, which means that the intention is not one of comparison or similarity between the wife/Lord and wife/husband relationship, but rather to indicate that part of the wife's relationship with her husband is to be identified with part of her relationship to the Lord. Second, both verses have feminine articular plural vocatives (αἱ γυναῖκες), imperatives are used (Col. 3.18) or intended Eph. 5.22 (see analysis of the ellipsis in v.22 above, pp. 25 ff.) and both contain references to husbands in the dative plural (with 5.22 adding ἰδίοις). In addition, the emphasis on integrating the vertical with the horizontal dimension seems to mitigate against the proposition that Col. 3.18 be understood as the only source for Eph. 5.22. For arguments against the appropriateness of the phrase "as is fitting in the Lord" for v.22 see my note 32 below.

are used) to conduct the household relationship as an essential part of that individual's relationship with "the Lord." There is no hint of challenging the integrity of the human to human relationship (i.e., the horizontal relationship) by insisting that such a relationship be conducted "as to the Lord."[32] It is precisely because this phrase allows for the possibility of integrating the two relationships (person to person with person to Lord) that it must be understood as constitutive for the argument of 5.22-24.

An analysis of the comparative particle ὡς confirms the above interpretation of the phrase "as to the Lord." Barth summarizes current exegetical opinion.[33]

First, ὡς can be interpreted as having a causal force in connection with the question of the wife's motivation. Barth cites both Col. 3.18 ("as is fitting in the Lord") and Eph. 5.21 ("in the fear of Christ") for contextual support of this interpretation.[34] At Eph. 5.21, 5.22 and Col. 3.18 ὡς is thought to signify cause and effect: the act of subordination is caused by specific motivation. They wife must be subordinate to the husband either *because* she fears the Lord (Eph. 5.21) or her husband (5.33) or because such is "fitting in the Lord" (Col. 3.18).[35]

The problem with this position is that Col. 3.18 is not the source for the phrase "as to the Lord" in Eph. 5.22, as I have argued above. Second, the question of motivation enters the discussion, but it cannot be based solely on the function of the comparative particle ὡς because, as

---

[32] The phrase "as is fitting in the Lord" (Col. 3.18) is avoided perhaps for two reasons. First, note that the appeal in Col. 3.18 is more to that which "is fitting" as distinct from focusing or directing the act *towards* the Lord. That is, Col. 3.18 intends to qualify the act of subordination as something that is acceptable, right or "fitting in the Lord". On the other hand, the phrase "as to the Lord" (Eph. 5.22; cf. 6.7; Col. 3.23) qualifies the wife's act of subordination teleologically by emphasizing the direction or orientation of the act. It must be directed *towards* the Lord. Second, the question of whether or not an act is "fitting in the Lord" does not lend itself to the analogies developed in vv.23-24. That is, the phrase has little potential for establishing a bi-dimensional frame of reference, a necessary element which makes possible the development of the analogies in vv.23-24. The phrase "as to Christ" is avoided perhaps on stylistic grounds. While Χριστός is used throughout Ephesians, κύριος does not occur until 4.5 and occurs most often in ch.5 (vv.8, 10, 17, 19, 22; but see also 6.4, 7, 8, 9). It appears that the term κύριος is restricted to the section on parenesis (chs. 4-6), and at 5.22 κύριος is favored over Χριστός.

[33] *Ephesians*, p. 612, n. 17 for the list of surveys which his own work summarizes.

[34] In addition, I would add that if motivation is the central thrust here then Eph. 5.33 should be included as well ("but let the wife fear the husband").

[35] BARTH, *Ephesians*, p. 612. Cf. MUSSNER, *Christus, das All und die Kirche*, pp. 50 (n. 1) and 148, who takes this position. Against this see CAMBIER, "Le grand mystère concernant le Christ et son Église," p. 64, ns. 1, 3, 4.

we have seen above, it functions primarily to link two distinct relationship (wife/husband with wife/Lord) by means of a single act of the
wife (i.e., subordination). The question of motivation must be inferred
from the context and thus seems to have a secondary role.

Moreover, the causal relationship between the act and its motivation is best connected with the ὅτι clause at v.23a ("*because* the husband
is head of the wife") and not with the phrase "as to the Lord." Finally,
the idea of that which is "fitting in the Lord" does not prepare the reader
for the analogies in vv.23-24 and therefore does not adequately fit this
context.

A second interpretation of ὡς shifts away from the question of
motivation and focuses on the act of subordination itself. Here the
concern is with the mode, integrity and radicality of subordination. The
wife is to be subordinate to the husband in exactly the same way that she
is subordinate to the Lord. Barth enlists the phrase "in everything"
(Eph. 5.24) in support of this position. In other words, there is no
difference between the wife's subordination to her husband and her
subordination to the Lord.[36]

According to my analysis below, the term κύριος can only refer to
Christ; only he is Lord of the wife, not the husband.[37] Yet the
implication of this second interpretation is that the wife must consider
her husband in *exactly* the same ways as she does the Lord. Moreover,
and as will be noted in my analysis of 5.23, the appositional phrase "he,
savior of the body" (5.23c) clearly distinguishes between the headship of
Christ and that of the husband. Thus, although points of contact do exist
between the wife's subordination to the husband and to the Lord, some
distinctions must be drawn in light of 5.23c.

Barth's description of the third position combines the questions of
motivation and comparison. He writes, "Subordination to Christ and
subordination to the husband are then as related and inseparable as are
the love of God and the love of man, or, perhaps as the love of neighbor
and the love of self." Barth finds that texts such as Mt. 25.40 may echo
this line of interpretation ("As you have done to one of the least of my
brethren, you did it to me").[38]

Whether Mt. 25.40 is what the author of Ephesians had in minds is
difficult to determine. Whether or not one can attribute a typological
role to the husband's headship or the wife's subordination — as Barth
speculates — is also difficult to ascertain. However, this last option is
promising for the following reasons.

---

[36] BARTH, *Ephesians*, p. 612.
[37] With Barth (Ibid., p. 613) and others.
[38] Ibid., p. 612, see same page for the fourth position.

First, this position admits a distinction between the wife's relationship with her husband and her relationships with the Lord. Logically, it is precisely because the two relationships are distinct that comparison becomes possible. The phrase "as to the Lord" seems to imply that although there is a difference between the wife/Lord and wife/husband relationships, they are nonetheless to be understood as intimately related by means of the wife's single act of subordination.

Second, as noted earlier, the comparative function of "as to the Lord" initiates a bi-dimensional frame of reference: the wife/Lord (vertical dimension) and the wife/husband (horizontal dimension) relationship. When we substitute cosmological categories (i.e., "earthly/ heavenly") for the geometrical ones used thus far in the chapter (i.e., "vertical/horizontal"), we find that the "heavenly" wife/Lord relationship is being integrated into the "earthly" wife/husband relationship. This pattern of integrating the two relationships helps us detect the integration of the two cosmological spheres and also serves as an illustration of a broader pattern present in vv.22-24 and Ephesians as a whole.

Two examples from Eph. 5 highlight this peculiar grammatical function of the comparative ὡς. The integration of the "heavenly" and the "earthly" spheres is accomplished by means of this comparative conjunction. In both 5.1 and 8 believers are depicted as "beloved children" (of God) (5.1) or as "children of light" (5.8). These depictions represent the basis upon which the ethics of this passage are built. For example, it is precisely because believers *are* beloved children of God that they must imitate their "Father"; it is precisely because they *are* "light in the Lord" (5.8) that they must walk as children of the light. In these two instances ὡς has a deictic function, denoting identity rather than simply comparison or similarity. Note that what is to be done on earth is determined or controlled "from above". The two spheres are integrated by means of the deictic function of ὡς which appears to link the ethical injunctions for life at the earthly level with the heaven-bound depictions of believers.[39]

The grammatical function of ὡς described above applies to v.22. The wife's one act of subordination integrates or links two spheres — the "earthly" and "heavenly" — as with the ethical injunctions of 5.1 and 8 based on the "light" and familial imagery. The text v.22 informs us that the wife's relationship with her husband is in some intimate way linked to her relationship with the Lord. In v.22 the integration of the two spheres is based on the injunction for subordination which is given a bi-dimensional focus with the phrase "as to the Lord."

---

[39] For the deictic function of ὡς see T. MURAOKA, "The Use of 'ΩΣ in the Greek Bible," *NovT* 7 (1964), p. 59.

In all three examples, the conceptual pattern of integration based on the grammatical function of ὡς suggests that at v.22 there are elements of the wife's subordination to the husband which, although remaining unspecified at the moment, should be identified with aspects of her subordination to the Lord.[40] In all three texts the author is not simply comparing or drawing parallels between the earthly and heavenly spheres, he is integrating them based on ethical exhortation. Certain elements of the wife's bi-dimensional existence (i.e., her relationship to the Lord and husband) are to be identified in the wife's one act of subordination.

How, then, does the phrase "as to the Lord" function on a conceptual level? Without first introducing the vertical or wife/Lord relationship to the wife/husband relationship, the headship (husband/ Lord) and subordination (wife/Lord) analogies of vv.23 and 24 would not follow from v.22. The phrase not only introduces a christocentric perspective (wife to Lord), it also establishes a bi-dimensional aspect to the wife's relational existence: according to v.22 the wife is related to both the husband and the Lord by means of her subordination.

This bi-dimensional aspect provides the conceptual frame of reference — the vertical and horizontal dimensions — for the address to the wives. By means of such a conceptual frame of reference the author prepares the reader for the analogies developed in vv.23-24. The author's creative and interpretative needs are adequately met with this phrase.[41]

In light of the bi-dimensional function of the phrase "as to the Lord" and the above interpretation of the comparative particle ὡς, I would argue that the Greek of v.22 might be paraphrased in the following manner: "Wives, be subordinate to your husbands, and consider this (act) an essential part of your relationship to the Lord." An analogy from mathematics might shed light on this paraphrase. The wife's relationship

---

[40] A determination of what is and is not identified between the wife/husband and wife/Lord relationship emerges in my last chapter.

[41] Let me point out that the integration of the horizontal with the vertical dimension indicates both the author's indebtedness to the tradition as well as his obvious freedom to modify that tradition. The kind of interpretive shift reflected in vv.22-24 — the integration of the two dimensions — also indicates the author's presupposition that the heavenly realm determines the ethical injuctions to be followed at the earthly level. That the author develops traditional materials throughout Ephesians is commonly held by exegetes. A good illustration of the similatities and differences between the *Haustafeln* texts of Ephesians and Colossians (which indicate some form of editorial activity) can be seen in Mitton's *Ephesians*, pp. 307-308 and Gnilka, *Epheserbrief*, pp. 21-29. Sampley's *One Flesh* remains one of the best English language form- and source-critical studies of 5.21-33 and provides ample witness to the use of Pauline and other traditional materials in the passage at hand.

with the Lord is the larger set which contains the subset of her relationship with her husband. Her act of subordination belongs to both sets, as it were. Yet in her one act of subordination to her husband she acts as one who is subordinate to the Lord and therefore is related to the Lord in a manner correlative to her married status. Only when the injunction is viewed from the larger set can definition and perspective be given to it in the subset. The above helps us to perceive that the wife relates to the Lord directly in her act of subordination. That is, her subordination is directly linked to the Christology presupposed in the phrase "as to the Lord."[42]

In summary, the ellipsis of the verb in v.22 alerts the reader that the author has given the injunction for subordination a nuanced meaning. The association of v.22 with v.21 by means of structure and grammar places the injunction for subordination in a christological context (v.21: "in the fear of Christ"; v.22 "as to the Lord") as well as in a context of living a life in the Spirit (the syntactical connection between 5.18 ["be filled with the Spirit"] and v.22).

This pattern of linking the sphere of the Spirit (i.e., "heavenly" sphere) with the sphere of human existence (i.e., the "earthly" sphere) in 5.1, 8, 18 ff. is continued with the phrase "as to the Lord" in v.22. This phrase establishes the vertical wife/Lord relationship while at the same time maintaining the integrity of the horizontal or wife/husband relationship. With this bi-dimensional frame of reference established, the

---

[42] This does not imply that the wife is to consider her husband as her Lord, as is clear when we examine the possible referents for the term κύριος. The question is: does the term refer to the husband or to Christ, or to both? Abbott (*Ephesians*, pp. 165-166) resolves the problem on grammatical grounds (as do others, see Barth, *Ephesians*, pp. 611-612 [with Abbott]; Cambier, "Le grand mystère concernant le Christ et son Église", pp. 63-64; against this position see those listed by Barth, *Ephesians*, p. 612, n. 17). At v.22 κύριος cannot refer to husbands nor to the husband and Christ since in either case the term would have to be in the plural to make grammatical sense. Nor can it refer just to the husband since κύριος does not point backwards to "husband." Rather, it has a proleptic function, preparing the reader for the modification of Christ's titles in v.23 ("head," "savior"). Therefore the term can only refer to Christ. However, we need to take into account my own analysis of the function of "as to the Lord." If the phrase is expressly used to initiate a vertical dimension to the wife's relational existence, then there can be no ambiguity about this phrase: κύριος refers to Christ. On the basis of grammar and context it is clear that the term must refer to Christ. If this is correct, then Sampley's opinion (*One Flesh*, p. 112) must be rejected. He writes, "There is nothing explicit within the passage that requires the exegete to reduce the ambivalence to a single meaning, which seems reason enough to allow the two-sidedness of its potential understanding to remain." However, with M. Dibelius, *An die Kolosser, Epheser an Philemon*, 3 Auflage (Tübingen: J.C.B. Mohr [John Siebeck], 1953), p. 93, and Schlier, *Christus und die Kirche*, p. 66, Sampley (p. 155) allows for a distinction between the headship of Christ and that of the husband, but not based on the phrase "as to the Lord" at v.23c, see note 44 below.

author can then develop the argument for the wife's subordination by
focusing on other aspects of the wife's relational existence: the nature of
the husband's headship (v.23) and the model of the church, which is
paradigmatic for the wife (v.24). Moreover, the phrase "as to the Lord"
extends the christocentric thrust of v.21 ("in the fear of Christ"). This
christocentric element in turn provides a basis and a focus upon which
the address to the wives can be theologically and structurally centered, as
we shall note in my analysis of v.23 which follows.

2. Eph. 5.23: a ὅτι ἀνήρ ἐστιν κεφαλὴ τῆς γυναικὸς
             b   ὡς καὶ ὁ Χριστὸς κεφαλὴ τῆς ἐκκλησίας,
             c   αὐτὸς σωτὴρ τοῦ σώματος·

At 5.23 the thought moves away from the act of subordination and
focuses on establishing the context within which the injunction to the
wife is given a broader base. The author creates this context by
introducing two analogies which, in his interpretation, exist between the
wife/husband and Christ/church relationship.

First he makes use of an analogy centered on the image of "head,"
which he applies to Christ and the husband (v.23). Second, he draws
another analogy to use for the church and wife, recalling the theme of
subordination (v.24). It is interesting to note within the address to wives
that the husband plays a central role, as do the church and, especially,
Christ. The author is very much concerned with drawing upon a number
of relationships with which he can then "map out" the address to the
wife.[43]

At v.23 the hypotactic conjunction (ὅτι) introduces the second part
of a three-pronged argument. Now that the wife's act of subordination to
the husband has been situated within a christocentric context (v.22), the
motivation for subordination as well as the wife's understanding or
perception of her husband is developed from that christocentric perspective.

As mentioned previously, the motivation for subordination is given

---

[43] This rather creative treatment of the *Haustafel* form is found only in Ephesians.
The author not only addresses the wife directly (v.22), he does so also in terms of her
relationship with her husband (v.23) and with the church (v.24). In vv.25-27 the husband
is addressed, in vv.28-29 the address is extended and developed, now in terms of his
relationship to his wife (she is perceived as being part of his own "body" etc.). The author
addresses both in terms of the other. Clearly the author is interested in addressing
relationships, in contrast to other *Haustafel* texts (Col. 3.18-4.1; 1 Tim. 2.8-15; Tit.
2.1-10; 1 Pet. 3.1-7) where only the wife — and not the wife with either the husband,
Christ or the church — is addressed. It seems clear that the author of Ephesians is
committed to specific traditional materials, as above, but exercises an obvious freedom in
terms of his modification of these materials. Below I shall pursue some of the reasons
why Christ plays such a dominant role in a passage which by design intends to address
wives.

at v.23a, which begins with the ὅτι clause. The wife is to be subordinate because her husband is "head." Applying the term "head" to the husband does more than provide motivation; it also prepares the reader for the analogy between the husband and Christ. That is, the term has two logical or structural functions. It provides one reason for subordination and also establishes the first part of an analogy which will lead to the image of Christ as "head," thus reinforcing the christocentricity of the injunction for subordination.

In terms of the analogy itself, the husband as "head" (v.23a: κεφαλή) is said to be like Christ (v.23b: κεφαλή). At this point in the text (vv.23a-b) there seems to be a direct parallel between the husband and Christ, as is indicated by the grammatical structure of vv.23a and b. The subject of v.23a (ἀνήρ) corresponds to the subject of v.23b (ὁ Χριστός). The copula at v.23a is understood at v.23b, resolving the ellipsis of the verb. Both vv.23a and b share the same predicate nominative (κεφαλή) and end with feminine genitive singulars. The parallels — conceptual and grammatical — between vv.23a and b are unmistakable and exact. According to the logic of the text, what is intended for the husband as "head" depends on what is intended for Christ as "head."

However, the appositional phrase at v.23c (αὐτός σωτὴρ τοῦ σώματος) clearly indicates that the husband's headship is to be distinguished from that of Christ: only Christ is said to be savior of the body.[44] Note that the wife's relationship to her husband is still determined "from above." She is linked to Christ not only by means of her act of subordination but also through the qualification given to her husband's headship, which is christocentrically defined (v.23b). Just as the wife's act of subordination is teleologically focused on Christ in v.22, at vv.23a and b she must perceive her husband's headship as being christocentrically determined.

The argument here is based on the understanding that there is some kind of link between the headship of the husband and that of Christ —

---

[44] Verse 23c must be taken as an appositional phrase qualifying Christ's headship, distinguishing between the headship of Christ and that of the husband on grammatical grounds. The antecedent for the masculine nominative singular αὐτὸς at v.23c can only be a masculine singular in v.23b. This leaves us with either κεφαλή or Χριστός. Since κεφαλή modifies the articular ὁ Χριστός, the only conclusion to be drawn is that the antecedent for αὐτὸς is ὁ Χριστός. The fact that αὐτὸς is singular eliminates the possibility, that both husband and Christ are intended. In this way two types of headship are distinguished, at least on a soteriological basis. Others argue this interpretation, see BARTH, *Ephesians*, pp. 614-617, who follows ABBOTT, *Ephesians*, p. 166; SAMPLEY, *One Flesh*, p. 125, who follows SCHLIER, *Christus und die Kirche*, p. 66; Idem, *Der Brief*, p. 254, n. 1. Cf. also GNILKA, *Epheserbrief*, p. 277 and n. 4 for others with whom he agrees. Against this position see MASSON, *L'Épître*, p. 211, n. 3.

and that *therefore* the wife must be subordinate to her husband.[45] But how does the first analogy develop the argument initiated at v.22?

At v.23 the argument now includes more than the notion that the wife's act of subordination to her husband is an essential part of her relationship with the Lord (v.22). The wife is related to the Lord not just through her action, but now through her perception of her husband as "head" (v.23a), a perception which is ultimately defined by Christ (v.23b). If the author had argued that the husband is simply "head" of the wife without linking this image to Christ as "head," he would have broken the vertical line between the wife and Christ established in v.22 and would have made the statement about being subordinate to the husband as "head," if not completely groundless, then at least dependent on some other line of reasoning.[46]

The critical link between v.22 and 23 is the vertical dimension initiated at v.22 ("as to the Lord") and developed in the headship analogy between the husband and Christ in v.23. Both the horizontal act of subordination (at v.22) and its horizontal complement (i.e., the husband as "head," v.23a) form two parts of the three-pronged argument which directs the wife's action to the Lord and defines her perception of the husband vis-à-vis the Lord (vv.23a, b).

3. Eph. 5.24: a ἀλλὰ ὡς ἡ ἐκκλησία ὑποτάσσεται τῷ Χριστῷ
                       b οὕτως καὶ αἱ γυναῖκες τοῖς ἀνδράσιν ἐν παντί.

The bi-dimensional dynamic initiated at v.22 and developed in v.23 continues at v.24. Although there is a shift of focus to the paradigm of the church's subordination as this relates to the wife, the author still maintains a christocentric perspective. The wife's act of subordination to the husband is not only made logically dependent on the church's subordination to Christ, it is also indicated grammatically in clear fashion (v.24a: ἀλλὰ ὡς; v.24b: οὕτως καί). Just as the church is subordinate to Christ (as "head"), so the wife must be with respect to her husband (also designated as "head").

The model of the church is paradigmatic for the wife precisely because of the church's subordination to Christ as "head" and "savior."

---

[45] Note that the issue of headship is based neither on the intrinsic superiority of the husband nor on any intrinsic inferiority of the wife (against MASSON, *L'Épître*, p. 211). Cf. 1 Pet. 3.7 for a statement about the "weaker sex." The issue in the text is one of defining or better, redefining, a known human phenomenon (wife/husband relationship) by means of a heavenly relationship (Christ/church).

[46] For example, there is another way of arguing about "headship," as in Paul's arguments in 1 Cor. 11.2-16.

In other words, *just as* (v.24a: ἀλλὰ ὡς) the church is subordinate to Christ, *so must* (οὕτως καί: v.24b) the wife be to her husband. The horizontal wife/husband relationship is now linked to the heavenly Christ/church relationship by means of the wife/church analogy. The christocentric focus is maintained: the wife must be subordinate to her husband as the church is to Christ (v.24). That is, the manner in which the church subordinates herself *to Christ* is determinative for the wife's subordination to her husband. As with v.22, at v.24 the wife's act of subordination is ultimately determined by being related to Christ, but now through the agency of the church's subordination to Christ.

Verse 24 represents the third part of the three-pronged argument. The church's subordination to Christ — as the model for the wife —maintains the vertical link between the wife and the Lord and also gives that act of subordination broader definition. Not only is the wife to perceive her relationship to her husband as being intimately connected to her relationship with the Lord, as is indicated in v.22 and illustrated by the analogy between her husband and Christ (vv.23a-b), in v.24 the church's subordination is paradigmatic for the wife. Even the church — as related to Christ — informs the wife's act of subordination to the husband.

In all three verses the vertical dimensions (wife to Christ) is present, containing a beginning (the wife) and ending point (Christ). The presence of the linking elements "head" (husband/Christ) and "subordination" (wife/church) as well as the analogies developed from them suggest the author's concern to maintain the integrity of the horizontal relationship while at the same time integrating and emphasizing the vertical link between Christ and the wife. The phrase "as to the Lord," with its intrinsic christocentric perspective, should be understood as the necessary element which provides the possibility for developing the two analogies in the text. The phrase also provides a theological direction — towards Christ — and a theological basis for the argument.

By way of summary, the following can be concluded about the logical structure present in vv.22-24. The author has developed a three-pronged argument. The presence of the phrase "as to the Lord" and the analogies developed create the bi-dimensional frame of reference within which the author can fashion his address to the wives. In doing so he situates the act of subordination within three distinct relationship. Although the address to the wife focuses on her act of subordination, the nuance given it reflects the author's concern for drawing relational lines between earthly and heavenly spheres. The wife's act of subordination to her husband is to be understood as being an intimate part of her relationship to the Lord (v.22). Her perception of the husband as "head" must have a christocentric focus (v.23). At v.24 the wife's act of subordination to the husband (and ultimately to the

Lord) is given further definition by means of the church's subordination to Christ. It is in this sense that the church's subordination is paradigmatic for the wife (v.24a).

Let me underscore the fact that the Christ/church relationship provides direction ("to the Lord"), perception (husband as "head" as Christ is "head") and example (church as paradigm) for the wife's act of subordination. The Christ/church relationship completely dominates the address to wives. More importantly, the logical structure — the three-pronged argument, the use of three relational lines, the use of analogies — of the address is such that every statement about the wife's subordination is dependent on a soteriological statement about Christ as "head and savior of the body" (v.23c). That is, soteriological and, more broadly, christological issues provide the theological points of focus for subordination.

C. Christocentricity and Eph. 5.22-24

There are a few peculiarities about vv.22-24 which deserve some comment and which when examined will confirm the christocentric nature of the "head/body" and "subordination" language in the text.

First, it is striking that the address to wives is dominated by a christocentric perspective. That all of the relational lines in the analogies begin with the wife is no surprise; that they all lead "up" to Christ, either by means of the wife's act (vv.22, 24b) or the husband as "head" (v.23) or even the paradigm of the church (v.24a) is striking in light of the absence of such a christocentric focus in other *Haustafeln* texts which address wives.

An examination of some of the structural features of vv.22-24 will indicate that 5.23c — a soteriological statement about Christ — is both the structural core and theological center of the address to the wives. This fact will raise some exegetical problems concerning the intention of the analogies developed in vv.22-24 and prepare a context for raising some concluding questions. To anticipate, the problems detected will force us to raise questions as to precisely how the heavenly "head/body" imagery relates to the husband and wife in light of the soteriological distinction of 5.23c.

From a structural perspective, we note that 5.23c is surrounded by carefully arranged parallel sentence structures. For example, vv.22 and 24b share almost identical vocabulary and syntactical features. Both contain an ellipsis of the verb and depend respectively on their previous linguistic units for their main verbal idea. Both have either the vocative (v.22) or nominative (v.24b) feminine plurals (αἱ γυναῖκες, identical inflections) followed by phrases in the dative plural (v.22: τοῖς ἰδίοις ἀνδράσιν; v.24b: τοῖς ἀνδράσιν) and singular (v.22: ὡς τῷ κυρίῳ v.24b: ἐν παντί). Thus, on the basis of vocabulary, grammar and stylistic considerations, vv.22 and 24b form parallel and external boundaries for the address to the wives. There are other parallels inside these boundaries.

Verses 23a-b and 24a bring us one step closer to the structural middle of the passage (v.23c). There exist a number of parallels between vv.23a-b and 24a.[47] However, crucial for our purposes is the way in which these verses relate to the logical structure of the text and to v.23c.

Verses 23b-24a form a chiasm which indicates that v.23c is indeed at the structural core. The subject of v.23b (ὁ Χριστός) becomes the object (τῷ Χριστῷ) of the present middle indicative (ὑποτάσσεται) at v.24a. The objective genitive of v.23b (τῆς ἐκκλησίας) becomes the subject of v.24a (ἡ ἐκκλησία). Except for the different verbs, v.24a reverses the order of the vocabulary in v.23b. Verse 23c, the soteriological statement about Christ, stands at the middle of the chiasm.[48]

It is instructive to relate the structural position of v.23c to the logical sequence of the text. Verse 23a introduces the first analogy ("headship"); v.23b completes it by linking the husband to Christ. The headship of Christ is then qualified at v.23c. This is followed by the second analogy ("subordination"), beginning with the church/Christ relationship (v.24a) and ending with the subordination of the wife (v.24b). In between the "head" (v.23) and "subordination" (v.24) analogies we find the soteriological statement about Christ who (as "head") saves the body (v.23c).

In other words, the headship analogy (vv.23a-b) leads to the soteriological statement at v.23c while the analogy between the wife and the church (v.24) follows it and is based on it. The soteriological statement at v.23c is "sandwiched" between the two analogies. It stands at the precise center of the logical sequence in vv.23-24.

That v.23c is the theological center of the passage is further confirmed by applying the categories of "heavenly" and "earthly" spheres to the text, and by paying special attention to the linking particle ὡς.

Both vv.23b and 24a begin with the same conjunction ὡς. At v.23b ὡς καὶ links v.23a ("because the husband is head of the wife") to v.23b ("just as Christ is head of the church"). At v.24a ἀλλὰ ὡς is somewhat

---

[47] For example, note that the copula in v.23a (ἐστιν) can supply the verbal idea for v.23b, just as the present middle indicative (ὑποτάσσεται) of v.24a supplies the verbal idea for v.24b. In this way vv.23a and 24a have parallel syntactical functions in that both furnish the verbal ideas for the linguistic units which follow them. I shall treat the rhetorical and structural aspects of vv.23b-24a in the next few paragraphs.

[48] For other chiastic interpretations see N.W. LUND, *Chiasmus in the New Testament: A Study of Formgeschichte* (Chapel Hill: The University of North Carolina Press, 1942), pp. 197-201, and SAMPLEY, *One Flesh*, pp. 122-123.

proleptic, anticipating the "return" to the earthly sphere by means of the wife/church analogy at v.24b (οὕτως καὶ: *"so also"* the wife [must be subordinate] to the husband in everything). Thus the flow of thought begins at the earthly sphere with the husband (v.23a), leads to Christ (vv.23b, c), remains in the heavenly sphere with the example of the church (v.24a) and then "returns" to the earthly sphere with the wife (v.24b). The heavenly sphere (vv.23b-24a) is completely encased by the earthly one (vv.22, 23a, 24b) and 5.23c is at the theological center.

The address to the wives is completely determined by the Christ/church relationship. Both structurally and rhetorically, the christocentric focus of the three-pronged argument is centered on v.23c. Everything in the passage, from the subordination of the wife and church to the headship of the husband is based, in a manner of speaking, on the image of Christ as "head" and "savior of the body."

This concern for christocentricity leads us to probe another peculiarity of the text — this is our final consideration — which concerns the intention of the analogies themselves.

I have argued that the appositional phrase "he, savior of the body" must be interpreted as distinguishing between the headship of the husband and that of Christ.[49] I also pointed out that what was intended for the husband as "head" was logically dependent on what was intended for Christ as "head."[50] When we allow for the soteriological distinction of v.23c, as the grammatical structure demands, we are left with a difficulty. If the husband is "head" of his wife just as Christ is "head" of the church (v.23a, b), but only Christ — and not the husband — is savior of the body (v.23c), then precisely how is the analogy to be understood? That is, exactly how is the husband "head" of his wife *just as* (v.23b: ὡς καὶ) Christ is "head" of the church? Beneath the surface of what appears to be a straightforward analogy between the husband and Christ there seems to be a more nuanced and complex association, which will require further discussion and analysis.[51]

D. **Conclusions**

The two considerations just mentioned — 5.23c as the structural and theological center of the address to the wives as well as the soteriological distinction between husband and Christ — lead to the following exegetical observations.

---

[49] See note 44 above.

[50] See my p. 38 above.

[51] Once the Christological nature of the "head/body" and "subordination" language is made clear in the chapter which follows, we shall then be in a position to determine the particulars of the nuanced association between Christ and the husband, in Chapter 5.

First, on the basis of my analysis of 5.22-24, it should be conceded that the author argues for the subordination of the wife by means of three distinct relational lines: (1) her relationship to the Lord (v.22), (2) her relationship to her husband (who is "head," v.23), (3) and her analogous relationship with the church (v.24). Therefore, any understanding of the wife's subordination must be determined in part from the three relational lines developed by the author.

Second, the three relational lines highlight the author's christocentric concerns. He reformulates the address to the wife so that all three relational lines and the analogies lead "up" to Christ. That is, the logical structures of the passage and of the analogies demand that any interpretation of the wife's subordination be developed in light of the soteriological and christological statements at v.23b-c. Therefore, according to the logical structure of the passage, any understanding of the wife's subordination must first begin with an analysis of Christ's role as "savior of the body," which will be the focus of the next chapter.

CHAPTER III

Adamic Soteriology

A. Introduction

The text of Eph. 5.31-32 makes clear that the citation from Gen. 2.24 applies first to Christ and the church, suggesting that Christ and the church — and not the wife and husband — are the primary referents of the σάρκα μίαν ("one flesh") relationship. The overall goal of this study is to demonstrate that the application of the "head/body," "savior" and "subordination" language to the Christ/church and wife/husband relationship (vv. 22-24) reveals the author's interest in connecting the wife/husband relationship to the New Adam/Eve σάρκα μίαν relationship of 5.31-32. The logical structure of 5.22-24 makes clear that what is understood for the wife/husband relationship is dependent on what is understood for the Christ/church relationship. The goal of the next two chapters, therefore, is to demonstrate that the application of the "head/body," "savior" and "subordination" language to the Christ/church relationship reveals the author's intent to reconstruct vv.22-24 in terms of Pauline and Jewish forms of theological reflection about Adam. We shall see that the author of Ephesians connects vv.22-24 to vv.31-32 by making use of language already associated either with Adam or Genesis within Pauline letters prior to Ephesians.

In the present chapter I argue that Christ's role as σωτήρ ("savior") at Eph. 5.23c must be interpreted in light of 2.14-18, where the author recasts the death of Christ on the cross in language echoing the first two chapters of Genesis. Therefore, or so I contend, the presence of the term σωτήρ at 5.23c is our first shred of evidence suggesting that the address to wives manifests a form of Adam speculation. Since I seek to demonstrate that the theological agenda guiding the expansion of Eph. 5.22-24 concerns Pauline and Jewish theological reflections about Adam's role in redemption, the analysis which follows will isolate the theological nature of Christ's role as "savior". In order to illustrate the necessity of such an approach, recall the debate between Sampley and Lincoln raised in the first chapter.

Sampley thinks that vv.31-32 influenced the construction of vv.22-24.[1] He argues that: (1) the presence of organic terminology at vv.23c,

---

[1] *One Flesh*, pp. 32-34, 113-116.

28-30 can be explained by appealing to the organic "one flesh" image at v.31; (2) there exists a widespread early Christian literary pattern which connects injunctions for subordination with texts from the Pentateuch.[2] Recall Lincoln's fundamental objection. Granted that texts such as 1 Cor. 11.8, 9; 1 Tim. 2.11-14 and 1 Pet. 3.5, 6 "all contain the verb ὑποτάσσω and ground the subordination in Torah,"[3] Eph. 5.22-33 does not fit such a pattern because in each of the above examples the "Torah text explicitly involves the notion of subordination. That is not the case with Gen. 2.24." For Lincoln, "subordination is not in view in this particular verse" because for him the point of Gen. 2.24 at Eph. 5.31 is the *mutual* "one flesh" relationship, not subordination.[4] The *subordination* of a "body" to a "head" has nothing to do with *mutuality* suggested by the "one flesh" imagery.

Lincoln's criticism can be challenged from a number of vantage points. According to Lincoln there is a chasm between what is said of Christ and the church at vv.22-24 and vv.31-32. If subordination has nothing to do with mutuality, then how does one explain that the church is subordinate to Christ (cf. v.24a) while at the same time involved in a relationship of mutuality with Christ (cf. vv.31-32)? It is because these two images are applied to the same Christ/church relationship throughout vv.22-32 that we must concede some relationship between subordination and mutuality.

Since Lincoln's objections touch upon the question of what images communicate, a comment about the use of imagery in Ephesians is in order. Lincoln's argument is based on an *a priori* assumption that the image of a "body" subordinate to its "head" cannot communicate the idea of mutuality depicted in the σάρκα μίαν image. As a general rule the basic logic of this position is quite sound, but Ephesians proves the exception.

The author of Ephesians is quite at ease with mixing one kind of image with another, perhaps with the intent of challenging his reader to consider carefully what is being communicated with reference to the church. The first mention of the church as a collection of believers is found in 1.22-23, where the feminine singular τῇ ἐκκλησίᾳ (v.22) is associated with the neuter singular noun σῶμα (v.23). In a similar way, at 5.28-29 the wife is associated with

---

[2] The critical texts are 1 Cor. 11.8, 9; 1 Tim. 2.11-14 and 1 Pet. 3.5, 6. See SAMPLEY, *One Flesh*, p. 97 (following C.K. BARRETT's work on this question in *A Commentary on the Epistle to the Romans* HNTC [New York: Harper and Row, 1957], p. 55) and p. 115 (following J.M. Robinson's detection of this pattern throughout the New Testament into the Apostolic Fathers, see "Die Hodajot-Formel in Gebet und Hymnus des Früchristen-tums," in *Apophoreta; Festschrift für Ernst Haenchen* [Berlin: Alfred Töpelmann, 1964], pp. 194-235).

[3] See LINCOLN, "The Use of the Old Testament," p. 35.

[4] Ibid., p. 36.

the husband's σώματα, σάρκα and very self. In both instances gender distinctions are linked or combined to form a composite image. A second example is found in 2.11-22. Here the unity of the church, especially between Jew and Gentile (vv.11-14), is depicted not in terms of the "head/body" imagery of 1.22-23 but in terms of the ἕνα καινὸν ἄνθρωπον (v.15: "one new human") and the ἑνὶ σώματι (v.16: "one body") language.[5] Yet at the end of chapter 2, the author discards the anthropomorphic image[6] and makes use of a constructional model. Beginning with v.19, the church is collectively called the "householders of God" (οἰκεῖοι τοῦ θεοῦ),[7] having a "foundation" (v.20: ἐπὶ τῷ θεμελίῳ), a "cornerstone" (v.20: ἀκρογωνιαίου) and a "structural quality" (v.21: οἰκοδομὴ).[8] Here the "building" image contains the quality of an organic or somatic image with the use of the verb αὐξάνω at v.21. The "building" just described is not only "being fit together" (v.21: συναρμολογουμένη), it actually "grows" (v.21: αὔξει) into a holy temple in Christ. Bodies grow, temples and buildings are constructed.[9] In this last instance we have a good example of mixing two metaphors.

The above examples taken together make clear that the author of Ephesians is quite comfortable with mixing his images.[10] The fact that an image related to buildings is also described as "growing" demonstrates that the author will apply a quality from one particular type of image, the

---

[5] Even though v.16 refers to Christ's body on the cross, this example still applies to the church because the adjective ἕνα suggests the unity of the church with the body of Christ.

[6] In line with the anthropomorphic imagery of 1.22-23 and 2.15, the author articulates the goal of the church's life in terms of the ἄνδρα τέλειον or "perfect man" (4.13).

[7] The term οἰκεῖοι does not refer primarily to buildings but to people. Even so, the term "householder" expresses the common denominator of a particular grouping of people: they all belong to the sociological grouping based on familial ties (in addition, slaves) with a common geographical component, namely, a house. In addition, note that at 2.22 the "householder" actually takes on characteristics of a building: believes are "constructed" (συνοικοδομεῖσθε) into a "dwelling place" or "abode" (κατοικητήριον).

[8] I readily acknowledge that at v.21 οἰκοδομὴ communicates edification or the notion of being built up and does not literally refer to a building *per se*. Even so, the fundamental properties of these terms are definitely derived from images having to do with buildings or edifices, cf. Mt. 24.1 and Mk. 13.1.

[9] Throughout the Pauline Corpus the use of the verb αὐξάνω ("to grow") occurs only when an organic or somatic image is being described, the exceptions being Eph. 2.21 and 2 Cor. 10.15. Cf. 1 Cor. 3.6-7 (God causes apostolic "seeds" to grow); 2 Cor. 9.10 (God causes the quantity of seed to grow); Col. 1.6 (the gospel bears fruit and grows); 1.10 (Christians are to bear fruit and grow in knowledge of God); 2.19 (the body grows because of its connection to the head), cf. Eph. 4.14. The cognate αὔξησις, found only at Eph 4.16 and Col. 2.19 in the New Testament, also suggests the notion of growth in terms of an organic or somatic image.

[10] In addition, images such as "head/body" (1.22-23; 4.15-16; 5.22-24), anthropomorphic images (2.15; 4.13) and nuptial imagery (5.31) all convey a single theme central to Ephesians, the unity of the church with Christ.

organic or somatic image, to a completely different image, the constructional image. It is reasonable to suggest that such is the case in vv.22-24 and vv.31-32. That is, there is ample reason to suggest that at vv.22-24 the subordination of the "body" to its "head" may have something to do with the mutuality of vv.31-32.

Even if Lincoln's objections must be rejected, the evidence for connecting vv.22-24 to the New Adam/Eve relationship at vv.31-32 is not overwhelming. Sampley's arguments concerning Pauline literary patterns and the similar function of generically related imagery are useful for analysis of the continuity of thought in Eph. 5.22-33 as a whole,[11] but they do not address the question of the literary and theological function of the "head/body," "savior" and "subordination" language cluster of vv.22-24. My contention is that the answer to the question of how the application of the "head/body," "savior" and "subordination" language of Christ and the church (vv.22-24) is related to Christ/church σάρκα μίαν relationship (vv.31-32) lies in a clear understanding of the literary and theological function of the language cluster at vv.22-24.

The analogical priority of the Christ/church relationship demands that any detection of Adamic Christology necessarily begin "from above." Granted the analysis must begin "from above," the question is, from which point: the subordination of the church (v.24b), the headship of Christ (v.23b) or the role of Christ as savior (v.23c)? There is little consensus on this question primarily because scholars are divided as to which of the two relationships is pre-eminent in vv.22-24.[12] Those who grant priority to the Christ/church relationship in vv.22-24 do not always take into account the logical structure of the text when interpreting the wife's subordination. The church's subordination to Christ is seldom given serious consideration.[13]

---

[11] In all fairness to Sampley, it must be said that one goal of his analysis is in fact to establish the continuity of thought throughout Eph. 5.21-33 as a whole.

[12] Recall Barth's comment, "Differing descriptions of the structure reveal whether the commentator attributes pre-eminence to the husband/wife topic or to the statements on Christ and the church." See *Ephesians*, p. 655.

[13] For example, Barth acknowledges that the Christ/church relationship is normative for what is said of the wife/husband relationship, cf. *Ephesians*, p. 652. Others agree, see HOULDEN, *Ephesians*, p. 332; SAMPLEY, *One Flesh*, pp. 103-108, 121-126; SCHNACKENBURG, *Der Brief*, pp. 252-253; MASSON, *L'Épître*, pp. 210-211. Yet Barth does not make use of this analogical feature of the text in his analysis of the wife's subordination in v.22. He is not alone in this regard, see HOULDEN, *Ephesians*, p. 332; SAMPLEY, *One Flesh*, pp. 121-126; SCHNACKENBURG, *Der Brief*, p. 252; MASSON, *L'Épître*, p. 211. In other words, the traditional approach analyzes v.22 by taking v.21 into account with no consideration given to v.24a-b. The single exception to the above might be E.F. SCOTT, *The Epistle to the Colossians, to Philemon and to the Ephesians* MNTC (London: Hodder and Stoughton, 1930). He argues that the wife and husband ought to live the kind of life articulated by Christ and the church, see pp. 237-238. This approach is certainly correct

Perhaps the neglect of the church's subordination (v.24a) is due to past preoccupation with the relationship of v.22 to v.21. There can be no doubt that v.21 relates grammatically to v.22. Clearly v.21 must be taken into account when analyzing the subordination of the wife.[14] My criticism of those who begin "from above" is that the logical structure of vv.22-24 is not taken into account when interpreting the subordination of the wife.[15] Any analysis which does not take into account the basic logical structure of Eph. 5.22-24 is handicapped long before the final results are in.

My suggestion is that the analysis must begin with v.23c ("he, savior of the body"). Recall that this verse stands at the structural and theological core of vv.22-24.[16] As an appositional phrase, v.23c qualifies v.23b ("just as Christ is head of the church") which in turn qualifies v.23a. Verse 23a in turn provides motivation for the wife's subordination ("because [ὅτι] the husband is head of the wife"). That is, the wife's subordination is linked to soteriology in two ways. The first concerns the wife/husband/Christ linkage. The second concerns the wife/church/Christ linkage. With regard to the first linkage, the noun "savior" qualifies Christ's headship which in turn qualifies the husband's headship. The husband's headship provides one of the motivating factors for subordination. The wife's subordination is clearly linked to the image of Christ as σωτήρ. With regard to the second linkage, the church's subordination to Christ is paradigmatic for the wife (cf. v.24). Since the church's subordination to Christ is qualified by Christ's role as "savior," the wife's subordination is linked to soteriology through the agency of the church. The term "savior" must be viewed as central to any analysis of the "head/body" and "subordination" language since this noun is like the first in a row of dominoes, affecting the other terms dependent on it.

In light of the above, the following approach is both warranted and necessary. The analysis must begin with the noun σωτήρ in v.23c because (1) it qualifies the image of Christ as κεφαλή in v.23b and (2) it directly qualifies the church's subordination to Christ (v.24a), the paradigm for the wife (v.24b).

---

to the extent that it is guided by the logical structures internal to the text, but he does not take into account the context of 5.18-21 as this relates to the ellipsis in v.22.

[14] Recall my arguments in the previous chapter. The participle ὑποτασσόμενοι at v.21 is the fifth of five participles dependent on the imperative πληροῦσθε at v.18. This particular grammatical construction at least suggests that the five distinct actions represented by the five participles (including "subordination") are to be linked with being filled with the spirit (v.18) which is also connected with ἐν φόβῳ Χριστοῦ (v.21).

[15] With the exception of SCOTT, *Ephesians*, pp. 237-238, whose analysis omits any consideration of 5.18-21.

[16] In the previous chapter I argue that the wife/husband relationship (vv.22-23a, 24b) completely encases the Christ/church relationship (vv.23c-24a), the theological and structural center of vv.22-24 being v.23c, "he, savior of the body."

B. Soteriology and Christology

Eph. 5.23   a ὅτι ἀνήρ ἐστιν κεφαλὴ τῆς γυναικὸς
            ὡς καὶ ὁ Χριστὸς κεφαλὴ τῆς ἐκκλησίας,
            αὐτὸς σωτὴρ τοῦ σώματος

The association of κεφαλή with ἐκκλησίας (v.23b) parallels the association of σωτήρ and σῶμα (v.23c). That is, Christ is depicted as "head" and "savior" of the "church," the "body." These terms occur individually elsewhere within the Pauline Corpus.[17] Yet nowhere else do they occur together as in vv.22-24.[18] The absence of κεφαλή, σωτήρ and σῶμα at Col. 3.18, the source for Eph. 5.22-24, indicates that the author of Ephesians is revising the injunction for subordination. The concentrated use of three terms to describe Christ (Χριστός, κεφαλή and σωτήρ, all within the last two thirds of one verse, v.23b-c) and the unparalleled association of these terms within Ephesians signal the author's intent to modify the address to the wives with several traditions (or fragments thereof) which — until the writing of Ephesians — were otherwise unconnected.[19] The question is, why is the author of Ephesians reshaping Pauline language? My contention is that, as with his unique use of the phrase "as to the Lord" (v.22), at v.23 the author reshapes language found in prior Pauline letters so as to connect the wife's subordination to Adam speculation. The first indication that Pauline language is being reshaped is the qualification of Christology (v.23b) soteriology (v.23c).

There can be no doubt that the author qualifies Christology with soteriology at vv.23b-c since Christ's role as "head of the church" (v.23b) is qualified by his role as "savior of the body" (v.23c).[20] It is striking that at Eph. 5.23b Christ's role as κεφαλή is qualified by his soteriological role (i.e., v.23c). Foerster takes note of this: at Eph. 5.23c, he says, "the

---

[17] For κεφαλή see, for example, 1 Cor. 11.3; Col. 1.18; 2.10, 19; the noun σωτήρ occurs only at Phil. 3.20 within the undisputed letters and it does not occur in Colossians; for σῶμα see 1 Cor. 6.12-20; ἐκκλησία is common enough.

[18] The "head/body" image relative to Christ and the church does not occur within the undisputed letters of Paul, but only in Ephesians (1.22-23; 4.15-16; 5.23) and Colossians (1.18 [cf. 2.9-10]; 2.19). The term σωτήρ does not occur with κεφαλή, σῶμα or ἐκκλησία within the Pauline Corpus as a whole.

[19] The unique combination of the four terms κεφαλή, ἐκκλησία, σωτήρ and σώματος has been noted by many. See GNILKA, Epheserbrief, p. 277 and SCHNACKEN-BURG, Der Brief, pp. 253-254. As we shall see, very few raise the question about the New Adam/Eve motif, and no one notes the congestion of titles which congregate at v.23.

[20] CAMBIER, "Le grand mystère concernant le Christ et son Église," p. 66; SCHLIER, Der Brief, p. 254; BARTH, Ephesians, pp. 614-616; SAMPLEY, One Flesh, p. 124; against the above see MASSON, L'Épître, p. 211, n. 3, who argues that v.23c should be attached to v.24 if ἀλλὰ is to make grammatical sense at v.24a.

κεφαλή quality does not include the σωτήρ quality."²¹ Unfortunately Foerster does not account for the qualification.²²

My contention is that Christ's role as σωτήρ represents the New Adam's role as creator of the New Eve, initially realized at the cross (2.15-16). In addition, the savior/creator role should be distinguished from the κεφαλή role since this second role involves a creative act on the part of God, who gives Christ as κεφαλή for the church, who then becomes the σῶμα of Christ (1.22-23). In other words, v.23b-c represents two distinct salvific acts on the part of God (who gives Christ as κεφαλή: 1.22-23; 5.23b) and Christ (with reference to his role as σωτήρ: v.23c). The use of v.23b-c to justify the subordination of the wife must therefore be understood in terms of the New Creation which comes about in Christ.²³

That .Christ's saving role represents the New Adam and that of creator needs to be demonstrated separately from the contention that Christ's role as κεφαλή is ultimately dependent on a creative act of God which gives Christ to the church. The remainder of this chapter focuses on Christ's role as σωτήρ.²⁴

C. Adamic Soteriology

What does it mean for Christ to be σωτήρ in Ephesians? More specifically, what is the theological understanding of this role? Many interpret v.23c in terms of v.25b ("just as Christ loved the church and gave himself up for her").²⁵ Differences notwithstanding, the general argument for this position is as follows. The presence of σωτήρ at v.23c introduces Christ's soteriological role. The nearest point of reference which defines or further specifies Christ's saving role is v.25b ("just as

²¹ W. FOERSTER, *TDNT*, VII, p. 1016, who follows SCHLIER, *Der Brief*, pp. 253-280 and J.T. Ross, *The Conception of ΣΩΤΗΡΙΑ in the New Testament* (Ph.D. Dissertation, University of Chicago, 1947), p. 250.
²² Schlier's speculation that the association between "head" and "savior" appears to be the author's defense against a competing interpretation which might intend to disassociate these two terms is intriguing (*Der Brief*, p. 254). However, since Ephesians is still "in search of a *Sitz im Leben*," it would be well not to speculate one way or the other about imagined or real opponents since there is little evidence for any conclusive results. Cf. R.P. MARTIN, "An epistle in search of a life-setting," *ExpTim* 79 (1968), p. 296.
²³ I readily acknowledge that the term "New Creation" is not found in Ephesians, cf. 2 Cor. 5.17. But a similar idea is expressed in different language throughout Ephesians, cf. 2.10, 15b; 4.13, 23-24.
²⁴ I begin with v.23c and not v.23b because, as I argue in the previous chapter, v.23c stands at the structural and logical center of the address to the wives. That is, the investigation must be guided by the internal features of the text.
²⁵ CAMBIER, "Le grand mystère concernant le Christ et son Église," p. 66; RAMAROSON, "L'Église," p. 139; GNILKA, *Epheserbrief*, pp. 277-279; SCHNACKENBURG, *Der Brief*, pp. 252-254; SCHLIER, *Der Brief*, pp. 254-257; MASSON, *L'Épître*, pp. 211-212; SAMPLEY, *One Flesh*, p. 125-128; HOULDEN, *Ephesians*, p. 333.

Christ loved the church and gave himself up for her"). Because v.23c is
further clarified at v.25b, it is concluded that Christ's saving role is linked
to his love for the church and his death on the cross.[26]

If we grant that v.23c points forward to v.25b, then we must ask how
Christ is able to save the church by loving her and giving himself up for
her? Scholars are not in agreement concerning the precise nature of
Christ's saving action at the cross. As Barth correctly notes, the term is
used within a number of secular and religious contexts contemporaneous
to Ephesians.[27] References to Hellenism[28] and Judaism[29] abound,[30] yet
most scholars are content to point out that within Ephesians the term
σωτήρ occurs within an *hapax legoumena*, "he, savor of the body"
(v.23c),[31] and thus limit their investigations to contrasting the eschatological function of the term in Eph. 5.23c with that of Phil. 3.20[32] or other
New Testament texts.[33]

The net result is twofold. First, most recognize that the use of σωτήρ
in Ephesians is distinctively different from its use in such texts as Phil.
3.20 and 1 Thess. 1.10. In all three texts Christ's role as savior is
described in terms of his role as God's heavenly agent.[34] But in Phil. 3.20

---

[26] That v.25b is a reference to Christ's death on the cross must be conceded at the
very outset. The evidence for this is incontestable. The occurrences of ἀγάπη and
παραδίδωμι with ὑπερ at Eph. 5.2 and 25b probably originate from Gal. 2.20, where
reference to the soteriological significance of Christ's cross is developed. The individual
use of ἀγάπη as a technical term for Christ's death (Rom. 8.37) and of παραδίδωμι for
the same function (Rom. 4.25; 8.32) further confirms that Eph. 5.2 and 25 draw on prior
Pauline language to develop the soteriological significance of Christ's death. For
literature see above note. On the distinctions between the apologetic and soteriological
uses of the παραδίδωμι tradition see especially N. PERRIN, "The Use of *(Para)didonai* in
Connection with the Passion of Jesus in the New Testament," in *idem, A Modern
Pilgrimage in New Testament Christology* (Philadelphia: Fortress Press, 1974), pp.
94-103.
[27] *Ephesians*, p. 616.
[28] SCHLIER, *Der Brief*, pp. 254-255; FOERSTER, *TDNT*, VII pp. 1004-1012.
[29] G. FOHRER, *TDNT*, VII pp. 1012-1013; FOERSTER, *TDNT*, VII pp. 1013-1015.
[30] See BARTH, *Ephesians*, p. 616, n. 31 for bibliography and literature.
[31] The phrase occurs only at Eph. 5.23c in the New Testament.
[32] The context of Phil. 3.17-21 is an important parallel to Eph. 5.22-24 because the
terms σωτήρ and ὑποτάσσω occur together only at Phil. 3.17-21 within the undisputed
letters of Paul. In addition, the term σωτήρ occurs only at Phil. 3.20 within the
undisputed letters. See RAMAROSON, "L'Église," p. 139; GNILKA, *Epheserbrief*, p. 277;
CAMBIER, "Le grand mystère concernant le Christ et son Église," p. 66; HOULDEN,
Ephesians, p. 333; SCHLIER, *Der Brief*, p. 254.
[33] The scholars listed below recognize that the term also occurs in the following New
Testament epistles with a decidedly different function than in Eph. 5.23c, cf. 1 Tim. 1.1;
2.3; 4.10; 2 Tim. 1.10; Tit. 1.3, 4; 2.10, 13; 3.4, 6; 2 Pet. 1.1, 11; 2.20; 3.2, 18; 1 Jn. 4.14;
Jude 25. See GNILKA, *Epheserbrief*, p. 277; CAMBIER, "Le grand mystère concernant le
Christ et son Église," p. 66; SCHLIER, *Der Brief*, p. 277.
[34] Phil. 3.20: ἐν οὐρανοῖς; 1 Thess. 1.10: ἐκ τῶν οὐρανῶν; for the heavenly function
of Christ as "head and savior" at Eph. 5.23b-c see 1.22-23.

and 1 Thess. 1.10 the chronological dimension differs from that of Eph. 5.23c. In the first two texts Christ's role as the "savior" from heaven takes place at a future time (i.e., at the *parousia*).[35] In Eph. 5.23c, and throughout the epistle, there is no reference to Christ's Second Coming.[36] Houlden observes that in the author's "vocabulary, Christ's already accomplished work is the 'saving' of his people and he is already their savior."[37]

Second, if most agree that in Ephesians the term σωτήρ articulates Christ's saving role as an ongoing reality, they do not agree as to precisely how Christ's death is salvific. Even the recognition of possible typological correspondances between the YHWH/Israel and Christ/ church relationship has not proven very helpful in this regard.[38] Within this approach, Christ saves the church by rescuing her.[39] The problem with this interpretation is that the context of 5.23c, 26-27 does not directly support the position.[40] With others, Schnackenburg contends that at v.23c Christ's role as savior must be interpreted in light of vv.25b-27, where Christ's love and death on behalf of the church as well as the results of this action are interpreted under the general rubric of soteriology. In this case Christ's saving action is understood in terms of

---

[35] 1 Thess. 1.10: ἀναμένειν. See CAMBIER, "Le grand mystère concernant le Christ et son Église," p. 66; SCHLIER, *Der Brief*, p. 277; GNILKA, *Epheserbrief*, p. 277.

[36] Believers *already have been blessed* by God in Christ (1.3: εὐλογήσας), *have already been made alive* with Christ (2.5: συνεζωοποίησεν). The use of the perfect passive participle σεσῳσμένοι at 2.5, 8 confirms that Christ's saving role is not futuristic but is perceived as already operative in the believer's faith life. See also 1.7: ἐν ᾧ ἔχομεν τὴν ἀπολύτρωσιν; 1.13: ἀκούσαντες ... πιστεύσαντες ἐσφραγίσθητε; 2.5: συνεζωοποίησεν, 2.13, and so on.

[37] *Ephesians*, p. 333.

[38] Cambier discovers a typological correspondence between Christ who saves the church (v.23c) and YHWH who saves Israel throughout the Prophetic corpus. In particular he detects a literary parallel between Hab. 3.18 (LXX) where YHWH is called "savior." The context of Hab. 3.18 (LXX) makes it clear that the saving action focuses on deliverance from and victory over the enemy. See "Le grand mystère concernant le Christ et son Église," pp. 23, 52-54, 6 and SCHLIER, *Der Brief*, p. 254 and HOULDEN, *Ephesians*, p. 333.

[39] E.g., HOULDEN (*Ephesians*, p. 333) agrees with Cambier, Christ's saving action is one of "rescuer," as with YHWH who rescues his people, see Dt. 32.15; 1 Sam. 10.19; Ps. 24.5 (LXX); in line with the notion of "rescuer," Scott translates Christ's role as "preserver" of the body, see *Ephesians*, p. 238; points of contact with Hellenistic Judaism are drawn by GNILKA, (*Epheserbrief*, pp. 277-287); see also SCHLIER, *Der Brief*, pp. 90-96.

[40] It is possible to conceive of Christ's love for the church and his death on her behalf in terms of "rescuing" her from sins. The primary evidence for this argument are the ἵνα clauses of vv.26-27. But since these clauses express the *results* and not the *manner* in which Christ's love and death saves the church, the argument is nugatory. The verbal parallel between Eph. 5.23c and Hab. 3.18 (LXX) indicates that Christ is given a soteriological role analogous to that of YHWH and nothing more. The significance of such an analogy will be treated in the following chapter.

Christ's agapic death.[41] This interpretation does connect the Christ's salvific action with his death on the cross. But there is no suggestion as to how Christ saves by loving and dying.[42]

P. Benoit connects the saving death of Christ with baptism: Christ saves through baptism. As evidence he points to the purity traditions mentioned in vv.26-27. In this instance the purification of the church is the primary saving action.[43] This interpretation does not take into account the grammar of vv.25b-27. The three ἵνα clauses of vv. 26-27 make explicit *the results* of Christ's love for and death on behalf of the church (v.25b). They do not express *the manner* in which his love and death saves the church. That is, the central question of how Christ saves the body (v.23c) centers on the action understood (5.25b) and not its results (vv.26-27).

If we follow the consensus and agree that v.23c points forward to v.25b (and vv.26-27), then Christ's role as "savior of the body" must be understood with reference to his agapic and self-giving death on the cross. Verses vv.25b-27 only make clear the conditions of Christ's death (v.25b: loving and self-giving) and the results of this death (vv.26-27). We must still determine the manner in which Christ's agapic death saves the church.

It is surprising that in their analysis of the term σωτήρ scholars are reluctant to draw connections between 5.23c, 5.25b (5.2) *and* 2.11-22. Why is 2.11-22 neglected? If 5.23c, 5.25b and 5.2 all refer to the cross, then certainly the most comprehensive treatment of Christ's death *on the cross* in Ephesians ought to be included in any analysis of these texts.[44] My proposal is that a careful analysis of the imagery and language in 2.11-22 will show that here Christ's death must be understood in terms of Adamic Christology and that understanding 5.23c in light of *both* 5.25b and 2.11-22 will lead us to detect the Adamic christological character of σωτήρ in 5.23c.

---

[41] *Der Brief*, pp. 252-253.

[42] Sampley connects the term with vv.25b-27 as well as 5.2. Christ's act of saving has to do with his death on the cross. See *One Flesh*, pp. 66-76, with MASSON, *L'Épître*, p. 211, n. 3.

[43] See, "Corps, tête et pléroma dans les Épîtres de la captivités," *RB* 63 (1956): p. 28.

[44] Perhaps the lack of interest in 2.11-22 is in part due to past preoccupation with history-of-religions questions. Echoes of this kind of question still surface, see the recent 1982 commentary by SCHNACKENBURG, *Der Brief*, pp. 253-254; GNILKA, *Epheserbrief*, p. 277, n. 7; SCHLIER'S, *Der Brief*, is an outstanding classic in this regard. Perhaps another reason is that scholars have been preoccupied with the surface structure of v.23b-c, (see P. BENOIT, "Corps", p. 23; RAMAROSON, "L'Église," p. 239; MASSON, *L'Épître*, p. 211, n. 3) or with Old Testament antecedents for the term σωτήρ (see CAMBIER, "Le grand mystère concernant le Christ et son Église," p. 66; SAMPLEY, *One Flesh*, pp. 3-60; HOULDEN, *Ephesians*, p. 333; BARTH, *Ephesians*, pp. 614-616, esp. 617).

Ephesians 5.23c, 5.25b and 5.2 relate to 2.14-18[45] thematically: all touch upon Christ's death on the cross.[46] Also, Eph. 5.23c can be linked to 2.14-18, especially vv.15-16, on the basis of vocabulary. Both texts address the Christ/church relationship with the term σῶμα. At 2.16 "the both" (τοὺς ἀμφοτέρους) are reconciled *in one body* to God through the cross" (ἐν ἑνὶ σώματι τῷ θεῷ διὰ τοῦ σταυροῦ). The parallel construction between 5.23b and c makes clear that the church (v.23b) is also the σῶμα (v.23c) of Christ. Both texts contain an unusual clustering of anthropomorphic imagery. At 2.15 we read "so that of the two he might create in him ἕνα καινὸν ἄνθρωπον" (lit.: "one new man"). At 5.23 we have another anthropomorphic image, the "head/body." If we compare other parts of 5.22-33 with 2.14-18, we see that both texts share other key terms: σάρξ (2.15; 5.29); ἐν (2.14, 15), μίαν (5.31).[47] There can be no doubt that 2.14-18 is related to the context of 5.22-33.

With the link between 2.15-16 and 5.23c in mind, we can now probe 2.15-16 for its Adamic characteristics and link these with 5.23c. Those who interpret 2.14-18 in terms of the New Adam motif focus on either the verb κτίζω or the noun ἄνθρωπος (both at v.15).[48] For example, Scott argues that at 2.15 the noun ἄνθρωποσ depicts Christ as the New

---

[45] Eph. 2.14-18 can be distinguished from vv.11-12 on the basis of material considerations. In 2.11-13 the pre-Christian status of believers is described, which is then followed by a description of Christ's soteriological function at vv.14-18. Then, in terms antithetical to vv.11-13, the status of believers is stated at vv.19-22 in light of salvation subsequent to the cross. See SCHLIER, *Der Brief*, pp. 122-127 and SMITH, "The Two Made One," pp. 43, 51.

[46] As indicated above, the use of ἀγάπη, παραδίδωμι and ὑπέρ at 5.2, 25b (cf. Gal. 2.20) are formalized references to Christ's death at the cross. At 2.16 we read that Christ made the two (or, both) one in one body to God "through the cross" (διὰ τοῦ σταυροῦ). As indicated above, the term σωτήρ at 5.23c points forward and so anticipates 5.25b.

[47] The following stylistical considerations are noteworthy. In both passages reflexive pronouns have somatic images as their referents. At 2.15 the referent for the reflexive ἐν αὐτῷ is ἐν τῇ σαρκὶ αὐτοῦ at v.14. (Why the author did not use the reflexive form ἑαυτῷ has vexed later copyists, for 2.15 see mss. D, G, Ψ etc.; at 2.16 ἑαυτῷ is once more substituted for αὐτῷ in mss. F, G and others; see also ABBOTT, *Ephesians*, p. 65.) The antecedent for ἐν αὐτῷ at the end of v.16 is ἐν ἑνὶ σώματι which occurs earlier in the verse. The effect of this grammatical feature is to multiply references to somatic imagery. In the space of vv.14-16 we can count five references to somatic imagery: (1) v.14: ἐν τῇ σαρκὶ; (2) v.15: ἐν αὐτῷ; (3) v.15: ἄνθρωπον; (4) ἐν ἑνὶ σώματι; (5) v.16: ἐν αὐτῷ. At 2.16 and 5.28 the noun σώματα is qualified by a reflexive pronoun, the pural genitive ἑαυτῶν. At 2.15 and 5.29 the term σάρξ is qualified by a reflexive, but now in terms of the singular ἑαυτοῦ. In both contexts reference is made to the male's body (at 2.15-16 with reference to Christ and at 5.28-29 with reference to the husband).

[48] Many do not raise the Adam question, see ABBOTT, *Ephesians*, pp. 63-64; SCHNACKENBURG, *Der Brief*, pp. 112-116; GNILKA, *Epheserbrief*, pp. 141-144; MASSON, *L'Épître*, pp. 166-167; SCHLIER (*Der Brief*, pp. 138, 90-96) makes reference to Jewish Adam speculation, but only in terms of the gnostic question.

Adam.[49] As the first Adam represents the whole human race at its beginnings, so the New Adam unifies all humans in the New Creation.[50] Houlden interprets the same noun with reference to Rom. 5.12-21, 1 Cor. 15.21-50 and Phil. 2.6-11, arguing that the connection between Christ and Adam is already within the Pauline tradition prior to Ephesians. But nothing by way of analysis is offered which might suggest concrete linguistic links to Eph. 2.14-18.[51] Smith is more specific in arguing that at 2.15 the term ἄνθρωπος probably echoes Gen. 1.27 (LXX), where the same term occurs.[52]

Links between Gen. 1-2 and Eph. 2.14-18 need not be restricted to the use of ἄνθρωπος at Eph. 2.15 and Gen. 1.27 (LXX). There is other evidence which supports a reading of Eph. 2.14-18 in terms of Adam speculation. An inquiry into the use of κτίζω (v.15) and ποιέω (vv.14-15) will be especially helpful. Let me state that the issue is not so much a question of finding parallel nouns and verbs — although this operation is critical — as it is a question of detecting the role which references to Adam play in the Pauline tradition. Therefore, the purpose of the following brief overview of Adam speculation in post-biblical Judaism and the undisputed letters of Paul is to situate the text of Eph. 2.14-18 within traditions centering on Adam. It is against the background of these traditions that the Adamic character of κτίζω (v.15) and ποιέω (vv.14-15) emerges.

Herman Gunkel's now classic *Urzeit* and *Endzeit* categories provide a useful tool for the following survey of relevant Jewish texts. Post-biblical Jewish interpreters often speculate about Adam's pristine and pre-fallen nature (i.e., *Urzeit*) in attempting to ground their speculations about the nature of "redeemed man" in the final days (i.e., *Endzeit*). There emerged many speculative theories as to what the nature of "redeemed humanity" would be like at the end of time. That is, God's intent for "redeemed humanity" is derived from the pristine pre-fallen status of Adam.[53]

---

[49] I take it that Scott assumes his reader understands that ἄνθρωπος occurs at Gen 1.26-27 (LXX) since he does not mention this detail in his analysis.

[50] *Ephesians*, p. 172.

[51] *Ephesians*, p. 291.

[52] SMITH, "The Two Made One," p. 43 and at p. 51 see n. 63; MUSSNER, *Christus, das All und die Kirche*, p. 87; HOULDEN (*Ephesians*, p. 291) concurs but also speculates that Ps. 80 might be involved as well. Cf. BARTH, *Ephesians*, p. 309.

[53] SMITH, "The Two Made One," p. 43 (following H. GUNKEL, *Schöpfung und Chaos in Urzeit* [Göttingen: Vandenhoeck und Ruprecht, 1895], pp. 367-371); N.A. DAHL, "Christ, Creation and the Church," in *The Background of the New Testament and its Eschatology*, eds. W.D. Davies, D. Daube (Cambridge: The University Press, 1956), pp. 442-443 and R. SCROGGS, *The Last Adam* (Philadelphia: Fortress Press, 1966), pp. 23-54.

Scroggs has shown that within apocryphal, intertestamental and rabbinic literatures Adam speculation articulates two basic and dominant themes. First, reference to Adam is made in terms of explaining the existence and origin of sin.[54] Second, Adam is often considered as embodying God's intention for all human existence.[55] Our concern is with this second theme. Scroggs outlines several ways in which Jewish post-biblical authors speculate about God's ultimate intention for fallen humanity vis-à-vis the first Adam. The dominant idea found is that the first Adam, in his glorious and pre-fallen state (i.e., *Urzeit*), will provide the model for "redeemed humanity" to be realized in the eschatological age (i.e., *Endzeit*). The attributes which interpreters see in "prefallen" Adam will be shared by "redeemed humanity" in the "age to come". As we shall see in a moment, Jewish Adam speculation is quite concerned with theological anthropology.[56]

Our first example is taken from the monarchical depictions of Adam. Adam is often depicted as a king,[57] whose reign over all of creation is initially expressed in the first two chapters of Genesis. Interpreters of these first two chapters develop the monarchical theme. According to them, Adam is also king not just of the earth and its animals, he is king over all other humans as well. Moreover, this *Urzeit* kingship will eventually be shared with all other humans after final redemption (i.e., *Endzeit*).

For example, the author of Wis. Sol. 9.1-3 relates the reign of ἄνθρωπος, (i.e., humankind) to Adam's rule over all creation found at 10.2. The point to note is that monarchical characteristics from Adam are transferred to all humans. The monarchical status of Adam at 10.2 — an interpretation of Gen. 1.26[58] — reflects God's intention for all of "redeemed humanity" subsequent to the fall.[59] Adam is the prototype for "redeemed humanity" in that he manifests God's original (*Urzeit*) and therefore God's eschatological (*Endzeit*) intent for redeemed humanity.

---

[54] *The Last Adam*, pp. 17-20 for apocryphal and intertestamental literature; for rabbinic literature see pp. 32-38.
[55] *The Last Adam*, pp. 21-31 for apocryphal and intertestamental literature and pp. 38-58 for rabbinic literature.
[56] This is the thesis of Scrogg's book, which is clearly set out *contra* others in the introductory chapter of *The Last Adam*.
[57] See Jub. 2.14; II Enoch 30.12; IV Ezra 6.53; Apoc. Mosis 24.4; etc.
[58] Gen. 1.26 (LXX) reads: καὶ ἀρχέτωσαν τῶν ἰχθύων τῆς θαλάσσης ("and let him be ruler over the fish of the sea") etc.
[59] SCROGGS, *The Last Adam*, p. 25. See also II Baruch 14-15 which amplifies this theme. Scroggs notes that Apoc. Mosis 24 witnesses to the loss of Adam's kingship.

Other examples exist within intertestamental and rabbinic literatures,[60] but a second example, taken from Qumran, suffices for illustrating the impact of the *Urzeit*-Adam on *Endzeit*-humanity.

Several passages from the Qumran scrolls contain the phrase *kol kabod 'adam* ("all the glory of Adam").[61] The example from 1QH 17.15 is most instructive. The beginning of the passage speaks of God's forgiveness of sins and his deliverance of all those who are corrected by God's judgements. Part of God's forgiveness is the reconstitution of human nature, as is clear from the following: "You will cause them [all humanity] to inherit *all the glory of Adam* and abundance of days." That is, restored humanity will receive specific characteristics — namely, glory — which are derived from the pre-fallen nature of Adam. Clearly Adam speculation within post-biblical Judaism develops eschatological anthropology (i.e., *Endzeit*) from what is thought to be the prefallen nature of the first Adam (i.e., *Urzeit*).[62]

The concern with eschatological anthropology or "redeemed humanity" is also found within the Pauline Corpus prior to Ephesians. Paul's interest in "redeemed humanity," however, is not derived from the first Adam (or the *Urzeit* pole), but from the last Adam, the resurrected Christ (i.e., the *Endzeit* pole).[63] For example, at Rom. 5.12-21 the implied typology between Adam and Christ serves to contrast the sin (vv.12-13) and death (v.14) of the first ἄνθρωπος (i.e., Adam) with the free gift of God's grace (v.15) and the believer's righteousness through Christ (v.17). Paul is not interested in the "pre-fallen" Adam as such because it is precisely in Christ's resurrected person that God's intent for all humanity can be found. The righteousness of the believer is granted through the Risen Christ. It is from and through the risen Christ — and not the pristine humanity of the first Adam — that believers receive God's grace. Human transformation occurs primarily through the instrumentality of the risen Christ.[64] From

---

[60] See SCROGGS, *The Last Adam*, pp. 25-27; W.D. DAVIES, *Paul and Rabbinic Judaism: Some Rabbinic Elements in Pauline Theology*, (Philadelphia: Fortress Press, [1948] 1981), pp. 44-57; E. SCHWEIZER, "Die Kirche als Leib Christi," pp. 241-256.

[61] SCROGGS (*The Last Adam*, p. 26) lists the following, 1QS 4.23; CD 3.20; 1QH 17.15.

[62] SMITH, ("The Two Made One," p. 43) points to 1 Enoch 85-90 as a prime example of this kind of thinking. Scroggs develops this motif in great detail within intertestamental and rabbinic literatures, see *The Last Adam*, passim.

[63] The Pauline tradition prior to Ephesians reflects a significant shift in Jewish Adam speculation. Within the undisputed letters of Paul, the model for redeemed humanity is no longer the Adam of Gen. 1-2 (*Urzeit* pole) but the Risen Christ (*Endzeit* pole).

[64] See especially 5.19b, 21b.

the perspective of the *Urzeit/Endzeit* pattern, the model for "redeemed humanity" — the resurrected Christ — is not drawn from the *Urzeit* pole. It is derived from the *Endzeit* pole.

The only other explicit comparison between Christ and Adam within the undisputed letters is 1 Cor. 15.21-22, 45.[65] This chapter addresses the problems believers in Corinth had with Christ's resurrection. The Adam/Christ typology is explicitly treated twice (vv.21-22, 45). In both cases the typology provides a context for understanding (1) Christ's resurrection itself and (2) the impact of this resurrection on believers. Once more the first Adam is contrasted with the eschatological Adam, Christ: "in Adam" all die, in Christ all shall be made alive (v.22). The first Adam became a living being, the eschatological Adam (ἔσχατος 'Αδὰμ) became a life-giving Spirit (v.45). Verse 48 makes clear that Christ — the heavenly one — is the paradigm for all those "who are of heaven."

That is, the resurrected Christ — and not the "pre-fallen" Adam — provides the paradigm for resurrected existence. There is no interest in the depiction of Adam found in Gen. 1-2. Paul focuses on the Adam of Gen. 3 and the following chapters to make clear that the resurrected person of Christ is the only source of eschatological hope for the life to come. In this instance Adam is linked to Christ by way of contrast. Adam functions negatively.

Christ's role as the *model* for "redeemed humanity" is clearest in terms of Paul's cautious treatment of the kind of "body" believes will have once they have been raised (vv.42-50). Paul contrasts the differences between human nature prior to and after the resurrection. That which is perishable will be imperishable, that which is weak will be powerful, etc. (cf. vv.42-43). The physical body will become a "spiritual body" (vv.44: σῶμα πνευματικόν). Verses 45-49 make clear that the "life-giving spirit" (v.45), the "one from heaven" (vv.47b, 48b, 49b), is the image which believers will bear in the resurrection (v.49: φορέσομεν καὶ τὴν εἰκόνα τοῦ ἐπουρανίου). Note that the model is of a spiritual type, in contrast to the "earthly" type: ὁ πρῶτος ἄνθρωπος 'Αδὰμ (v.45: "the first man, Adam"). That is, the use of ἄνθρωπος with reference to Adam functions negatively, in contrast to the spiritual "heavenly one."

---

[65] I do not wish to imply that Rom. 5.12-21 and 1 Cor. 15.21-22, 45 are the only passages where Adam plays a significant role. I restrict my analysis to these two texts because they are the clearest illustrations of Paul's thinking on Adam. D.M. Stanley illustrates the importance of Genesis throughout the Pauline Corpus, see "Paul's Interest in the Early Chapters of Genesis," *Studiorum Paulinorum Congressus Internationalis Catholicus*, AnBib 17-18 (1963): 241-252. See also A.J.M. WEDDERBURN, "Adam in Paul's Letter to the Romans," *Studia Biblica* III (1978): 413-430.

In Jewish Adam speculation the figure of "Adam" represents the hope for "redeemed humanity." However, Paul's belief in the resurrected Christ forces him to modify the pattern. For Paul, the resurrected Christ fulfills and embodies those eschatological features anticipated in "redeemed humanity." Paul must therefore begin his description of God's intent for "redeemed humanity" from the *Endzeit* pole represented in the person of Christ since he is the initial realization of eschatological humanity.

The author of Ephesians develops Pauline Adam speculation, but in a manner more consistent with the pre-Pauline Jewish speculation briefly examined above. At Eph. 5.31 the text of Gen 2.24 (LXX) is quoted, followed by v.32: "this mystery is great, but I speak concerning Christ and the church." Verses 31-32 modify Pauline Adam speculation from two perspectives. First, reference is now made to both Adam *and* Eve, not just Adam. Second, the text of Gen. 2.24 functions positively. It represents a return to the *Urzeit/Endzeit* pattern found in, for example, the Qumran texts cited above. That is, the author of Ephesians considers the "one flesh" union of the first Adam and Eve in their pre-fallen status (i.e., *Urzeit*) as an appropriate point of reference for interpreting the *Endzeit* Christ/church relationship. Here there is no negative contrast as with the typological arguments of Rom. 5.12-21 and 1 Cor. 15.21-22, 45.

In a manner consistent with the treatment of Gen. 2.24 (Eph. 5.31-32), at Eph. 2.15 the term ἄνθρωπος also functions positively, describing the Christ/church relationship with reference to the creative work of Christ's cross. At Gen. 1.26-27 the term ἄνθρωπος represents all humanity. Its universal application makes ἄνθρωπος a particularly apt term for describing the unity between all Gentiles and all Jews who are in Christ (Eph. 2.11-21). Just as the Jewish interpreters prior to Paul "provide details" absent from Gen. 1-2 in their interpretations of Adam (and Eve), so the author of Ephesians describes the existence of the "new anthropos" in terms of the peace made by Christ as well as the resulting reconciliation to God.[66]

---

[66] Note that the *Urzeit/Endzeit* categories are not restricted to anthropomorphic imagery. In Eph. 1.4 we learn that God chose believes "in Christ" before He created the cosmos *to be holy* (ἁγίους) *and blameless* (ἀμώμους) *before him in love* (ἐν ἀγάπῃ). If we can call the holiness, blamelessness and love "pre-fallen" characteristics of God's intent for redeemed humanity, then these become realized with the union between Christ and the church, the first sign of redeemed humanity at 5.25b-27. What was God's intent ἐν ἀγάπῃ in 1.4 becomes Christ's total gift of self and life to the church in 5.25 (ἠγάπησεν). The holiness and blamelessness of those he chose before the creation of the cosmos (1.4) become characteristics of redeemed humanity at 5.26 (ἁγιάσῃ) and especially 5.27 (ἁγία καὶ ἄμωμος). That is, even non-organic or non-anthropomorphic vocabulary illustrate the author's obvious interest in the *Urzeit/Endzeit* pattern found in Jewish forms of Adam speculation: God's protological intention for holiness and blamelessness (1.4) is fully realized in the historical action of Christ's love and care for the church (5.25-27).

The presence of the verbs κτίζω and ποιέω at Eph. 2.15 represent unique developments within Pauline Adam speculation. The objection against interpreting κτίζω as creation-centered language is that this verb does not occur at Gen. 1-2.[67] However, the argument that κτίζω involves this sort of language need not be restricted to references from Gen. 1-2. At Gen. 14.18-21 the verb κτίζω (vv.19, 22) depicts God as creator *and* deliverer (i.e., savior) from enemies. The same verb is used at Ps. 88.12 (LXX) (cf. vv.10-14), where God once again is depicted as creator, this time of north and west. The author of Matthews uses the participle ὁ κτίσας (lit.: "the creating-one" or "he who created") with reference to God's making of Adam and Eve at Gen. 1.27.[68] At 1 Cor. 11.9 ἐκτίσθη is used to describe the creation of woman (or Eve) through man (or Adam). Clearly this verb expresses God's role as creator without direct reference to the first two chapters of Genesis.

At Eph. 2.15, Christ is the subject of κτίζω. The association of this verb with Christ is significant because this verb is restricted to God elsewhere in the Greek scriptures. In other words, in Ephesians Christ is now given a direct creative role in fashioning the New Creation.[69] Christ is not only the New Adam of the New Creation, he is also, for the first time in the Pauline Corpus, directly involved in what was restricted to God — the act of creating.[70] The presence of ποιέω at Eph. 2.14-15 signals a clear verbal link back to Gen. 1-2 and also reinforces the New Adam's active role in creating the New Creation. In both creation accounts of Genesis the verb ποιέω expresses God's intent to create humanity (ἄνθρωπος). In the first account both the intent to create (Gen. 1.26) and the action of creating (1.27) are expressed with the verb ποιέω. In the second account ποιέω expresses only the intent to create (2.19).

---

[67] The absence of κτίζω in Gen. 1-2 has not deterred others from arguing that its use at Eph. 2.15 still refers to Genesis, see HOULDEN, *Ephesians*, p. 291 and MASSON, *L'Épître*, p. 166, n. 4.

[68] After the New Testament period the verbs ποιέω and κτίζω may have been synonymous. At Mt. 19.4 the preferred reading for God is ὁ κτίσας (Codex Vaticanus, Codex Koridethi) while ὁ ποιήσας is found in Codex Alexandrinus and Codex Ephraemi.

[69] Others make note of this, see BARTH, *Ephesians*, p. 308.

[70] According to 2.10 believers are created by God in Christ. Here the verb κτίζω refers to God's activity in Christ. Whether this verb refers to God as sole creator who creates through Christ (thus delegating Christ to an instrumental function, as is the consistent pattern throughout the Pauline letters), or whether this verb anticipates 2.15 is not something that touches upon the core of my argument since at 2.15 clearly only Christ — and not God — is the subject of the subjunctive κτίζω. However, when 2.10 and 2.15 are taken together, the implication is that Christ does not usurp God's role but simply shares it: he is co-creator with God.

The use of this same verb at Eph. 2.14-15 reinforces the creative aspect of the New Adam's salvific death. At v.14b the articular aorist ὁ ποιήσας functions as a substantive, providing further specification to the statement "he is our peace" (v.14a).[71] That is, Christ is the believer's peace in that he is "the-one-making" (ὁ ποιήσας) "the two" (i.e., Jew and Gentile) one. Just as YHWH "makes" humanity (ἄνθρωπος) at Gen. 1.26-27, Christ "makes" both Jew and Gentile as one. The results of this creative activity are expressed in the ἵνα clause at v.15: ἵνα τοὺς δύο κτίσῃ ἐν αὐτῷ εἰς ἕνα καινὸν ἄνθρωπον ποιῶν εἰρήνην. Here the participial phrase ποιῶν εἰρήνην is dependent on the aorist subjunctive κτίσῃ. In effect, two verbal ideas which interpret Christ's saving death are either directly related to God's role as creator in Gen. 1-2 (ποιέω: Gen. 1.26, 27; 2.19) or to God role as creator found in other texts (κτίζω: Gen. 14.19, 22; Ps. 88.12).[72]

The author of Ephesians merges what is properly a theo-logical action — namely, the act of creating — with what is properly a soteriological and christological action — Christ's death on the cross. The typological correspondance between YHWH and Christ should not be understood in terms of "deliverer" or "rescuer" alone. The image of Christ depicted at 2.14-15 represents the New Adam who now shares in the divine act of creating. The New Adam is not simply the eschatological model for "redeemed humanity," but is also its co-creator.

The question is now: how is the New Adam the model for redeemed humanity? The author of Ephesians follows the Pauline tradition at v.15 by providing a christocentric answer to this question. The making of the two into one (v.14b) as well as the creating of the one new anthropos occurs ἐν αὐτῷ, namely in Christ (v.15). The dative singular ἐν αὐτῷ can be either masculine (meaning: "in him" or "in himself") or neuter singular (meaning: "in it"). If it is masculine, the phrase probably has a reflexive force and translates "in himself" or "in his person," with reference to the person of Christ.[73] The ἵνα clause of v.15 then reads: "so

[71] Many note the role of Is. 57.19 (LXX) at Eph. 2.13-18. Whether vv.13-18 represent a traditional hymn, the author's own interpretation of Is. 57.19 or his interpretation of a hymn perhaps underlying Col. 1.15-20 are issues not directly relevant to the present discussion. The most recent treatment of these and other problems can be found in LINCOLN, "The Use of the OT in Ephesians," pp. 25-30 and n. 37.

[72] J. COUTTS ("The Relationship between Ephesians and Colossians," 201-207) argues that the presence of συζωοποιέω at Eph. 2.5 (elsewhere only at Col. 2.13) may reflect the New Adam motif since its cognate ζῳοπ ιηθήσονται occurs at 1 Cor. 15.22 and 45, where the Adam/Christ typology is clearly being developed.

[73] Most of the recent commentators follows this line of thinking, see BARTH, Ephesians, pp. 264, 295-297; ABBOTT, Ephesians, p. 65; SCHLIER, Der Brief, pp. 134-135; SCHNACKENBURG, Der Brief, pp. 115-116; GNILKA, Epheserbrief, pp. 142-143; MASSON, L'Épître, p. 166. The reflexive force of ἐν αὐτῷ vexed later copyists, who "corrected" v.15 with ἐν ἑαυτῷ, see Codex Vaticanus², D, G, Ψ and the Majority text.

that *in himself* he might create the two as one new ἄνθρωπος, making peace." If the phrase is neuter, then the antecedent for ἐν αὐτῷ is probably ἐν τῇ σαρκί (v.14), and the text reads: "so that *in his flesh* he might create the two as one new anthropos, making peace."[74] In this instance the creation of the one new anthropos occurs in Christ's "flesh." Either way, the creation of the one new anthropos begins with and in Christ, the New Adam. Christ is not just the "model" for "redeemed humanity"; through his life-giving death and in his very person or flesh he creates "redeemed humanity."

The author of Ephesians recasts Christ's death on the cross in patterns parallel to Pauline and Jewish Adam speculation. The significant development here is Christ's role as co-creator of "redeemed humanity." Christ's work as savior of the body (5.23c) alludes to the beginning of this relationship, when Christ creates the church from his very own self or flesh (2.14-18). Because the terms ἄνθρωπος, ποιέω and κτίζω allude to God's creative role in the Greek scriptures and are applied to Christ's saving death at 2.14-18, they represent the *Endzeit* pole within Adam speculation. In this way they establish the eschatological or *Endzeit* function of the Christ/church relationship: together they represent God's intent for "redeemed humanity" in the "final days." The text of 2.14-18 represents the genesis, if you will, of renewed humanity in Christ.

D. Conclusions

In answer to our initial question — what is the theological understanding of Christ's role as σωτήρ at 5.23c — the above analysis clearly illustrates that the language of v.23c ("he, savior of the body") is rooted in the author's own interpretation of Adam speculation. At 2.14-18 he breaks with Pauline tradition and links Christ with the role of the Creator found in the first two chapters of Genesis. The presence of the *hapax legoumenon* at v.23c ("he, savior of the body") prompts the reader to recall the New Adam/Eve relationship of 2.14-18 and anticipates the text of 5.31-32.

With regard to the link between 5.23c and 2.14-18, the noun σωτήρ refers primarily to Christ's action on the cross (v.25b),[75] and ultimately to his creative death (2.14-18). Because the noun σωτήρ refers to the creation of the "one new anthropos" (2.14-18), it signals the initial beginning of redeemed

---

[74] This reading is based on the presence of ἐν αὐτῷ at Eph. 2.15 in mss. P⁴⁶, Codex Vaticanus*, A, B, P, etc.

[75] As a reference to the cross, the noun evokes a number of images: Christ's love for and self-gift to the church (5.25b) and the result of his saving actions on the church (5.26-27).

humanity, where believers are incorporated into Christ's very self or "flesh" (2.15: ἐν αὐτῷ). In short, the presence of σωτήρ (5.23c) points forward to 5.25b, which recalls the creative death of the New Adam at 2.14-18. The justification for subordination given at v.23c is rooted in Adam speculation.

We have already noted that the author is at ease mixing his metaphors. In light of this literary technique, it is quite reasonable to suggest that the image of the "one new anthropos" of Eph. 2.15 expresses in the language of Gen. 1.26, 27 (i.e., ἄνθρωπος; cf. also Gen. 2.19; ποιέω: 1.26, 27; cf. 2.19) what Eph. 5.31-32 expresses in the language of Gen. 2.24 (i.e., σάρκα μίαν).[76] That is, both texts express the same eschatological relationship, but in different imagery.

The link between Eph. 5.23c and 5.31 is based on the presence of σῶμα (5.23c) which establishes that Christ and the church are as "head" and "body" at vv.22-24. It also prepares the reader for the analogies of vv.28-29 (which also make use of somatic imagery) and ultimately for the organic "one flesh" imagery of 5.31. Because it anticipates the "one flesh" relationship of the New Adam and Eve at 5.31-32, the noun σῶμα also signals the presence of Adam speculation.

The association of σωτήρ with σῶμα at 5.23c brings into sharp focus that Christ's role as savior is deeply rooted in the language and theology of Pauline Adam speculation. At v.23c two Adamic themes intersect, giving that verse a double referent: (1) the initial creation of the organic Christ/church relationship expressed in terms of Adam speculation (i.e., ποιέω, ἄνθρωπος and κτίζω) and (2) the organic "one flesh" relationship of the New Adam and Eve expressed at 5.31-32.

The ensuing realization is that the wife's subordination is now being linked to something quite new, to "redeemed humanity," the New Creation, the "one new anthropos," or, to the "one flesh" relationship represented by the New Adam/Eve (2.14-18; 5.31-32). Within such polyphonic references, the statement "he, savior of the body" ultimately communicates Christ's co-creative role in the formation of the church: Christ's death saves the church by first creating it.

---

[76] The text of Gen. 2.24 is used at Eph. 5.31 because of the *Haustafel* form, see SAMPLEY, *One Flesh*, pp. 97-102.

CHAPTER IV

Adamic Headship & Subordination

A. Introduction

Two other shreds of evidence which indicate that the injunction for subordination manifests a form of Pauline theological reflection about Adam are the term κεφαλή and the restricted application of ὑποτάσσω to the church (Eph. 5.24a). My contention is that both of these elements are linked to Adamic Christology prior to Ephesians (1 Cor. 11.3: κεφαλή; 1 Cor. 15.28b: ὑποτάσσω) and that their presence in Ephesians represents a modification of the kind of Adam speculation found in the undisputed letters of Paul. The Adamic nature of the language is eschatological in intent; therefore these terms express final saving actions of God and Christ which bring about the New Creation. We shall see that the ultimate justification for the wife's subordination to the husband's headship is properly theological, his role as "head" represents an act of God who gives the husband to the wife. The use of this kind of language also represents the author's way of exhorting the wife to enter into the process of salvation — by means of subordination — which points toward what is achieved by Christ and the church (the New Adam and Eve) at 5.31-32: "one flesh" unity.

B. The Pauline use of ΚΕΦΑΛΗ Prior to Ephesians

The association of the "head/body" imagery with Christ and the church occurs only in Colossians and Ephesians.[1] The ecclesiological use of "body" and the christological use of "head" occur within the undisputed Pauline letters.[2] Thus most scholars grant that the "head/body" language in Ephesians in related to Pauline sources prior to Ephesians.[3]

---

[1] See Col. 1.18; 2.19; Eph. 1.22-23; 4.15-16; 5.23.

[2] For κεφαλή see 1 Cor. 11.3; for σῶμα see 1 Cor. 12.12-13 and Rom. 12.5.

[3] Abbott (*Ephesians*, p. 166) links Eph. 5.23 to 1 Cor. 11.3, as do other, cf. S. Bedale, "The Meaning of κεφαλή in the Pauline Epistles," *JTS* 5 (1954):211-215; BENOIT, "Corps," pp. 25, 29; MASSON, *L'Épitre*, p. 211, n. 2; GNILKA, *Epheserbrief*, pp. 276-277 and SCHLIER, *Der Brief*, p. 253; *idem*, *TDNT*, III, p. 679. Below I argue that the "head/body" association of Ephesians is drawn from Col. 2.18, but the interpretation of that language is influenced by 1 Cor. 11.3. and 1 Cor. 15.20-28.

Scholars generally recognize that even if Ephesians were not pseudepigraphic, the language found there can be assessed and understood against the dominant religious and intellectual currents of the day. The language and worldview of Ephesians is seen to overlap with a number of Biblical, Hellenistic Jewish, popular philosophical and medical intellectual currents contemporaneous with Ephesians.[4]

However, we must not lose sight of the fact that at Eph. 5.22-24 the the author of Ephesians is expanding a Pauline text — the address to wives found at Col. 3.18 — with Pauline[5] and other traditions.[6] In addition, because scholars have underestimated the impact of Gen. 2.24 on the expansion of Eph. 5.22-24, they seldom consider whether Pauline theological reflections about Adam could have influenced the address to wives. Therefore, points of contact between Eph. 5.22-24 and the undisputed letters of Paul need to be examined afresh with our question in mind. In what follows I shall establish (1) that the noun κεφαλή (Eph. 5.23) and the verb ὑποτάσσω (Eph. 5.24a) are connected to theological reflections about Adam found elsewhere in the Pauline Corpus and therefore prior to their use in Ephesians and (2) that the theological reflection about Adam which Paul initiates is adopted and adapted by the author of Ephesians at 5.22-24.[7] If I can demonstrate these two points, then we shall have sufficient evidence to suggest that the

---

[4] For example, Colpe ("Leib-Christ," p. 181) argues that Philo's modification of the Stoic *Logoslehre* represents a clear enough cosmological function of the term κεφαλή that one can explain the use of the term in Ephesians in terms analogous to that of the Alexandrian Jewish interpretive traditions (cf. *De spec. leg* III. 184; I. 147; *De praem. et poen.* 114; *Leg alleg.* I. 12; I. 96); see also GNILKA, *Epheserbrief*, p. 276. Aside from Jewish-Hellenistic sources, Sampley (*One Flesh*, p. 64-65), following the work of W.L. KNOX (*St. Paul and the Church of the Gentiles* [Cambridge: Cambridge University Press, 1939], p. 161), acknowledges that the author of Ephesians creatively utilizes traditions of organic terminology which were pervasive in hellenized Judaism and which were commonplace in popular Hellenistic philosophy (cf. Seneca's *Epistulae Morales* 95,51; *De Clementia* i.5.I). Smith ("The Two Made One," pp. 34-35) makes clear the connections between Eph. 2.14-18 and Jewish proselytizing language contemporaneous to Ephesians. Aside from popular philosophy, Barth (*Ephesians*, pp. 186-192) and Benoit ("Corps," p. 27) suggest that the notion of a "head" guiding, giving life to, and, being the source of a "body" may have originated from Hellenistic medicine contemporaneous to Ephesians.

[5] E.g., SCHANACKENBURG, *Der Brief*, p. 251; HOULDEN, *Ephesians*, pp. 332-335.

[6] See Käsemann's now classic statement in which Ephesians is depicted as a mosaic of traditional materials in his "Ephesians and Acts," p. 288; see also Sampley, *One Flesh*, p. 1.

[7] The question as to what prompted the author to link Christ and the church with the text from Gen. 2.24 can in part be explained by reference to 1 Cor. 6.16, where that text describes the relationship between Christ and the individual believer with regard to sexual immorality. Precisely what prompted the author to develop this idea one step further by linking Christ and the church to the wife/husband relationship is entirely another matter. Two promising approaches, both of which link the thought world of

theological agenda guiding the expansion of Eph. 5.22-24 is in part rooted in Pauline interpretations of the first two chapters of Genesis.

The critical Pauline sources for understanding the use of the κεφαλή/σῶμα association at Eph. 5.23b-c; 4.15 and 1.22 are 1 Cor. 11.2-16; Col. 1.18; 2.10 and 2.19. The text of 1 Cor. 11.3-7 in part accounts for the structural context of Eph. 5.23. The texts from Colossians account for the "head/body" association.[8]

The text of 1 Cor. 11.2-16 is important for two reasons. First, its importance lies not only in the fact that here Paul alludes to the first two chapters of Genesis in connection with men and women. Paul does this elswhere, as Stanley points out.[9] In particular, it represents the only instance in which Paul connects Gen. 1-2 with the term κεφαλή, as we shall see below.[10] Second, when viewed from the perspective of Eph. 5.22-24, the connection between κεφαλή and Gen. 2.24 at 1 Cor. 11.2-16 may very well represent a Pauline precedent which establishes — for the author of Ephesians — a theological precedent which connects Gen. 2.24 with κεφαλή and male/female relationships.

At 1 Cor. 11.2-16 Paul takes up the question of women's roles and their proper headdress within the context of Christian worship at Corinth.[11] Vease 3 provides the foundation for Paul's arguments in the rest of the passage. Here he outlines the hierarchical structure God/Christ/men/women centered on the noun κεφαλή. He then applies this structure to vv.4-6, which results in the understanding that a man ought not to cover his head at the worship service while a women should. At v.7 Paul recalls the noun κεφαλή, connecting it with εἰκών which alludes to (LXX) Gen. 1.26 where the same term occurs.

Ephesians to the writings of Philo of Alexandria, are Colpe, "Leib-Christ," pp. 181-187 and R. WILD, "'Be imitators of God': Discipleship in the Letter to the Ephesians," Chapter 6 in *Discipleship in the New Testament*, ed. F.F. Segovia (Philadelphia: Fortress Press, 1985).

[8] Those listed below include 1 Cor. 11.3 and any combination of the three texts from Colossians listed above: ABBOTT, *Ephesians*, p. 166; BARTH, *Ephesians*, pp. 183-184; Bedale, "The Meaning of κεφαλή," pp. 211-215; BENOIT, "Corps," pp. 25, 29; CAMBIER, "Le grand mystère concernant le Christ et son Église," pp. 49-50; GNILKA, *Epheserbrief*, pp. 276-277; MASSON, *L'Épître*, p. 211 and n. 2; SCHLIER, *Der Brief*, p. 253; *idem*, *TDNT*, III, p. 679.

[9] E.g. 1 Cor. 6.16. See "Paul's Interest in the Early Chapters of Gensis," pp. 241-252.

[10] Within the undisputed Pauline corpus, κεφαλή occurs at Rom. 12.20; 1 Cor. 11.3 (3x), 4 (2x), 5 (2x), 7, 10; 12.21; within the disputed letters see Col. 1.18; 2.10, 19; Eph. 1.22; 4.16; 5.23 (2x).

[11] That the nouns ἀνήρ and γυνή need not be interpreted as "husband" and as "wife" is cogently argued by H. CONZELMANN, *1 Corinthians* (Philadelphia: Fortress Press, 1975), p. 184, who points out that in vv.12-16 Paul's concern is with questions of community worship and not marriage. Cf. SCHLIER, *TDNT* III p. 679.

Most would agree that the association of κεφαλή whith εἰκών does not mean that Paul is interpreting the text of Gen. 1.26. Rather, he is working with an interpretation of Genesis which is mediated through Hellenistic Jewish thought.[12] The point to stress, however, is that the fundamental frame of reference underlying his interpretation of male/female relationships at Corinth is rooted in the text Gen. 1-2. The notion of "man" as the "image and glory" of God (1 Cor. 11.7) and the notion that woman was made from man (v. 8) themselves suggest come contact with the first two chapters of Genesis.[13] The important point for this study is that the term κεφαλή is applied to Christ and husband in a context which associates the term with references to the creation accounts of Gen. 1-2. Clearly the term κεφαλή is linked with a type of theological reflection about Adam within the undisputed Pauline Corpus prior to the writing of Ephesians.

The importance of 1 Cor. 11.2-16 for interpreting Eph. 5.23 becomes evident when the material and conceptual points of contact between 1 Cor. 11.3 and Eph. 5.23 are examined. The parallels are as follows:[14]

1 Cor. 11.3:

[13] Θέλω δὲ ὑμᾶς εἰδέναι
ὅτι
παντὸς ἀνδρὸς ἡ κεφαλὴ ὁ Χριστός ἐστιν
κεφαλὴ δὲ γυναικὸς ὁ ἀνήρ
κεφαλὴ δὲ τοῦ Χριστοῦ ὁ Θεός

---

[12] The precise form of Jewish speculation about Genesis and Adam with which Paul is engaged is not at issue here, nor does it directly impinge upon my arguments concerning Ephesians *per se*. For a discussion of this see CONZELMANN, *1 Corinthians*, pp. 182-191, SCHLIER, *TDNT*, III, p. 679, and JERVELL, *Imago Dei*, pp. 100-104.

[13] A number of commentators detect connections between Gen. 1-2 and 1 Cor. 11.3, see C.K. BARRETT, *Corinthians*, HNTC (New York: Harper and Row, 1968), p. 248; W.F. Orr and J.A. WALKER, *1 Corinthians*, AB 32 (Garden City, N.J.: Doubleday and Company, Inc., 1976), pp. 262-263; A. Robertson and A. PLUMMER, *A Critical and Exegetical Commentary on the First Epistle of St. Paul to the Corinthians*[2] , ICC (Edinburgh: T. & T. Clark, 1914), p. 299; CONZELMANN, *1 Corinthians*, p. 187.

[14] Many note the relationship between Eph. 5.23 and 1 Cor. 11.3: Schnackenburg (*Der Brief*, p. 251) readily admits that the author of Ephesians stands within the tradition of 1 Cor. 11.3 and modifies it. Abbott (*Ephesians*, p. 166) considers 1 Cor. 11.3 as the critical parallel to Eph. 5.23. Sampley (*One Flesh*, p. 81) contends that the tradition about Christ's headship at 1 Cor. 11.3 is "developed in a creative new way" at Eph. 5.23, cf. Bedale, "The meaning of κεφαλή," p. 214; GNILKA (*Der Brief*, p. 276) speculates that 1 Cor. 11.3 may provide the conceptual model for the analogies at Eph. 5.23. Unfortunately none of these authors make clear precisely how the texts from Ephesians are to be linked to the pertinent texts from the undisputed letters of Paul.

Eph. 5.23a-b:

[23a] ὅτι
ἀνήρ ἐστιν κεφαλὴ τῆς γυναικὸς
ὡς καὶ ὁ Χριστός κεφαλὴ τῆς ἐκκλησίας

It is not difficult to see how the author of Ephesians modifies the language of 1 Cor. 11.3 by that of Colossians. Instead of Christ being head of all men (1 Cor. 11.3) Christ is head of the church (Eph. 5.23b; Col. 1.18). At 1 Cor. 11.3 the man is head of the woman while at Eph. 5.23a-b the husband and Christ are respectively the head of the wife (Eph. 5.23a) and of the church (Eph. 5.23b).

In addition, Eph. 5.23 maintains the overall conceptual design found in 1 Cor. 11.3. In 1 Cor. 11.3 the cosmos is depicted as having two levels, the heavenly realm of God and Christ and the earthly sphere of men and women. The link between the two spheres (God/Christ to men/women) and the links within the spheres (God to Christ, men to women) are based on one and the same term, κεφαλή. Clearly the spheres overlap. At Eph. 5.22-24 a similar picture is presented. The husband and wife form the earthly level, Christ and the church the heavenly level. Once again the term κεφαλή links both levels (v.23a-b: wife/husband, Christ/church) and the elements within each level (v.23a: husband to wife; v.23b: Christ to church). In all likelihood the conceptual structure of Eph. 5.23-24 is drawn from 1 Cor. 11.3, a text which the majority acknowledge is connected to the text of Gen. 1-2, as we have seen.[15]

But the debt to 1 Cor. 11.3 is not restricted to the use of key vocabulary. The structure of the analogies at Eph. 5.23-24 follow the cosmological and anthropological patterns of 1 Cor. 11.3. The application of the term κεφαλή to Christ not only defines Christ, it also defines the man (1 Cor. 11.3) and the husband (Eph. 5.23a) in terms of Christ. Thus the way in which men and husbands are related to Christ is strikingly similar in both Eph. 5.23a-b and 1 Cor. 11.3. The relational parallels between the two texts, not to mention the presence of the noun κεφαλή, indicate that the language and structure of Eph. 5.23 are closely linked to the context of 1 Cor. 11.2-16, where the term κεφαλή is associated with (LXX) Gen. 1.26. The impact which 1 Cor. 11.3 has had on Eph. 5.23a-b suggests that the theological agenda guiding the expansion of the address to wives is based in part on Paul's interpretation of the first creation account.

We must now account for the "head/body" association. The points

---

[15] God is not mentioned, but 1.19-23 makes clear that God is above since he is the one who works through and in Christ throughout this passage, thus suggesting his position above Christ.

of contact between Eph. 1.22-23; 4.15-16 on the one hand Col. 1.18; 2.10, 19 on the other account for the "head/body" association within Ephesians as a whole. The argument proposed by many is as follows. Although the terms "head" and "body" appear separately within the undisputed Pauline letters, their association together occurs only in Ephesians and Colossians. Since Colossians is generally thought to have been written before Ephesians, the proposal is that Ephesians draws the "head/body" configuration or imagery from Colossians.[16] The parallels are:

(1)
[18]   καὶ αὐτός ἐστιν ἡ *κεφαλὴ* τοῦ *σώματος* τῆς *ἐκκλησίας*

Eph. 1.22-23:
[22]   καὶ αὐτὸν ἔδωκεν *κεφαλὴν* ὑπὲρ πάντα τῇ *ἐκκλησίᾳ*
[23]   ἥτις ἐστιν τὸ *σῶμα* αὐτοῦ τὸ *πλήρωμα* τοῦ τὰ πάντα ἐν πᾶσιν πληρολμένου
(Cf.   Col. 2.10: καὶ ἐστὲ ἐν αὐτῷ *πεπληρωμένοι* ὅς ἐστιν ἡ *κεφαλὴ* πάσης ἀρχῆς καὶ ἐξουσίας.)

Eph. 5.23b-c:
[23b]   ὡς καὶ ὁ Χριστὸς *κεφαλὴ* τῆς *ἐκκλησίας*
[23c]   αὐτὸς σωτὴρ τοῦ *σώματος*

The noun κεφαλή maintains its first position in all three texts, but the last two nouns are in reverse order in Eph. 1.22-23 and 5.23b-c: first κεφαλή, followed by ἐκκλησία (1.22) or ἐκκλησίας (5.23b) and then σῶμα (1.23) or σώματος (5.23c). The perfect πεπληρωμένοι of Col. 2.10 becomes πλήρωμα at Eph. 1.23. The tightly constructed ἡ κεφαλὴ τοῦ σώματος τῆς ἐκκλησίας of Col. 1.18 is diffused at Eph. 1.22 by the addition of the prepositional phrase ὑπὲρ πάντα and the relative pronoun ἥτις at 1.23. What is clear from these brief observations is that the author of Ephesians in expanding the language of Colossians by adding qualifications not necessary at Col. 1.18.

---

[16] The dependence of Ephesians on Colossians has long been noted. MITTON (*Ephesians*, p. 57) points out that of the 2,411 words in Ephesians, 26.5% have verbatim parallels in Colossians. Of the 1,570 words in Colossians, 34% or more than one third of them appear in Ephesians. The statistical and other evidence suggest that Ephesians is in part dependent on Colossians. Others argue this, see Dibelius, *An die Kolosser*, p. 64; ABBOTT, *Ephesians*, p. xxiii; COLPE, "Leib-Christ," p. 174. GNILKA represents current thought on the relationship between Ephesians and Colossians, see his *Epheserbrief*, pp. 7-13. Against this see Coutts, "The Relationship between Ephesians and Colossians," pp. 201-207 and W. Munro, "Col. iii.18-iv.1 and Eph. v.21-vi.9: Evidences of a Late Literary Stratum?" pp. 434-447.

(2)   Col. 2.19:
[19]   καὶ οὐ κρατῶν τὴν *κεφαλήν* ἐξ οὗ πᾶν τὸ σῶμα...
       συμβιβαζόμενον αὔξει τὴν αὔξησιν τοῦ Θεοῦ

Eph. 4.15-16:
[15]   ... ὅς ἐστιν ἡ *κεφαλή* Χριστός [16] ἐξ οὗ πᾶν τὸ σῶμα
       ... συμβιβαζόμενον ... αὔξησιν τοῦ σώματος

The phrase ἐξ οὗ πᾶν τὸ σῶμα at Col. 2.19 is verbatim at Eph. 4.15 except for the anarthous Χριστός. The verb συμβιβάζω and the noun αὔξησις are inflected in exactly the same fashion in Col. 2.19 and Eph. 4.16. These two examples support the contention that the association of the "head" with the "body" found in Ephesians originates with Colossians.[17]

Granted the literary dependency of Ephesians upon Colossians with regard to the "head/body" association, it does not necessarily follow that Ephesians is dependent on Colossians in its *use* of the language drawn from it. The context of Colossians as a whole makes clear that the "head/body" language articulates Christ's superior cosmological position as Lord over the whole universe (1.15-18; reiterated at 2.10), especially over the heavenly powers. Here the language links the church to Christ (as a body to its head) to support an argument against angel worship.[18] At v.19 the author warns his readers that those who worship angels and not Christ do not hold "fast to the head, from whom the whole body, nourished and knit together through its joints and ligaments, grows with a growth from God." In this instance the "head/body" imagery functions polemically, illustrating what is not achieved by those who worship angels.

No such polemic against angels or elemental spirits is found at Eph. 4.15-16. The context of 4.1-16 suggests that the grace (4.7, 11) Christ gives to the believers leads them to a unity of faith (4.13). This unity builds up the body into a "mature manhood" (4.13: ἄνδρα τέλειον). Christ is the standard or measure (4.13) and source of that growth (4.15-16). There is no hint of polemic against the worship of angels.[19].

---

[17] That is, assuming the two documents are not dependent on a common source which they modify independently of each other. Since no such source has been uncovered or suggested (like the so-called "Q" document postulated in the two-source hypothesis), and, since the parallels between Colossians and Ephesians are so close, at times even exact, my tendency is to think in terms of literary dependency rather than a common tradition being interpreted variously.

[18] See BENOIT, "Corps," p. 24.

[19] This is not to say that Ephesians is not without its polemics. Certainly 4.15 could be interpreted as some form of polemics. Of course the problem is to determine the context for this polemic (if present) since the actual *Sitz im Leben* is still undetermined.

It should be clear that the author of Ephesians draws the "head/body" language from Colossians and interprets it in light of 1 Cor. 11.2-16 at Eph. 5.23a-b. But, how did the author connect these two traditions? The answer to this question will provide further evidence that at Eph. 5.23a-b the term κεφαλή expresses Pauline theological reflection about Adam. We shall see that the "head/body" language found throughout Colossians has great potential for expressing Pauline theological reflections about Adam's role in salvation.

C. The Sematic Range of ΚΕΦΑΛΗ in Ephesians

Scholars agree that in Ephesians the term κεφαλή communicates a fundamental idea about Christ, namely, his absolute Lordship.[20] At 1.22-23 the same term links Christ to the cosmological powers as well as to the church: Christ has been given as "head over all things for the church" (v.22). Since the same term connects Christ to two relationships[21] without drawing any distinctions between the two relationships, scholars suggest that there are at least two meanings for the term in Ephesians.

The text of Eph. 4.15-16 specifies the kind of Lordship Christ exercises within the Christ/church relationship. Here the "head" is the "source" from which (4.15: ἐξ οὗ) the body grows. The use of κεφαλή to express Christ's absolute Lordship over all (1.22) and to express the idea that Christ is the "source" of the church's growth supports the contention that the term has a double meaning.[22] However, this use of κεφαλή is peculiar to Colossians and Ephesians. As an expression of social and

----

[20] CAMBIER, "Le grand mystère concernant le Christ et son Eglise," pp. 58-59; SCHLIER, *Der Brief*, p. 89, n. 1; GNILKA, *Epheserbrief*, pp. 276-277; SCHNACKENBURG, *Der Brief*, p. 79; BENOIT, "Corps," pp. 23-25.

[21] He is over "all things," (1.22: [τα] πάντα) which includes all "authority" (1.21: ἀρχῆς), all "power" (1.21: ἐξουσίας), all "might" (1.21: δυνάμεως) and angelic powers (1.21: κυριότητος, see, for example, SCHNACKENBURG, *Der Brief*, pp. 74-80). His position as κεφαλή also includes his Lordship over the church (1.22). A. van Roon (*The Authenticity of Ephesians*, p. 216) has shown that πᾶν/τά πάντα represents a comprehensive concept referring to all created things prior to and during the New Testament period.

[22] This line of thinking is common enough, see SCHLIER, *Der Brief*, pp. 89, 200, 253-254; *idem, TDNT*, III, p. 680; Cambier, "Le grand mystère concernant le Christ et son Église," pp. 49, 59; GNILKA, *Der Brief*, pp. 276-277; BARTH, *Ephesians*, p. 614. G. HOWARD ("The Head/Body Metaphors in Ephesians," *NTS* 20 [1974], p. 353) is certainly correct in pointing out that this passage stresses the overall headship of Christ, which encompasses the hostile cosmological powers and the church. But, as the semantic range of the term κεφαλή suggests, he is certainly incorrect in rejecting a double meaning for the term. As will be clear in what follows, Christ relates to the church as its source of life (4.15-16) as well as its groom (5.31-32). He does not relate to hostile cosmological forces in this fashion. See Best, *One Body in Christ*, pp. 146-147; BARTH, *Ephesians*, p. 184.

political solidarity, the "head/body" imagery is commonplace in Antiquity.[23] However, the notion of "head" meaning both "Overlord" and "source" of the "body" is not found in classical, post-classical or Hellenistic Jewish sources.[24] In addition, the only New Testament texts which state that the κεφαλή is the "source of growth" for the σῶμα are Col. 2.19 and Eph. 4.15-16.

The fact that the "head/body" association occurs for the first time in the Pauline Corpus in Colossians and then in Ephesians coupled with the double meaning of κεφαλή strongly suggest that Colossians and Ephesians represent a unique development of Pauline thinking about the Christ/church relationship. What prompted this association in the first place? My contention is that the flexible semantic range of κεφαλή represents a major factor to be considered. An examination of the wide semantic range of κεφαλή in the Greek Scriptures makes clear that this word has great potential for expressing a number of related theological themes, not the least of which is Pauline reflection about Christ and Adam.

Bedale's work on the semantic range of κεφαλή offers useful insights which explain how the "head" can be the source of life for the body. Within the Hebrew Bible the noun rōsh ("head") has a broad semantic range. It can have an anatomical meaning[25], or a meaning derived from the literal sense as in the "top" of a mountain[26] or hill[27] and so on. A second principal value centers around the notion of "first," as in the first of a series.[28]. Certainly the notion of "head over" as in "social authority" is related to this second meaning. In texts such as 1 Chr. 5.12; 23.8, 11 (cf. Jud. 11.11) the meaning of "beginning" gives way to the meaning of "priority" as with "authority" in social relationships. The point of interest to us is how these meanings of rōsh are rendered in the Greek Scriptures.

The translators of the Septuagint often interpret the Hebrew rōsh with either ἄρχων and ἀρχηγός.[29] At times κεφαλή (cf. Jud. 11.11; 2

---

[23] This point is well documented by KNOX, *The Church of the Gentiles*, pp. 160-163.

[24] Both BARTH (*Ephesians*, p. 191) and BENOIT ("Corps," p. 27) recognize the parallels between Ephesians and Hellenistic medical sources, Scripture and popular philosophy. In my opinion they are justified in rejecting these as direct sources for the notion of the "head" as source of the "body's" growth. At best the neurological system described by Galen is only analogous to the "head/body" association in Colossians and Ephesians.

[25] Bedale does not cite any examples, but I have found the following: Gen. 40.16-17; Dt. 21.12; Num. 5.18.

[26] See Gen. 8.5; Ex. 19.20.

[27] See Ex. 17.9; 2 Sam. 8.25.

[28] BEDALE ("The Meaning of κεφαλή," p. 212) lists Mic. 1.13 (the beginning of sin); Prov. 1.7 (of knowledge) and Gen. 1.1 (the beginning of the world).

[29] Ibid., p. 213.

Sam. 22.44) or ἀρχή (cf. Ex. 6.25; Mic. 3.1) are preferred. Bedale points out that when *rōsh* is being translated, ἀρχή and its cognates are sometimes synonymous with κεφαλή. The only clear illustration of the synonymous relationship between these two terms is at Is. 9.14-15. At v.14 the phrase "head [Heb = *rōsh*] and tail" is rendered as κεφαλὴν καὶ οὐρὰν while at v.15, where this phrase is explained, *rōsh* is translated by ἀρχή. Bedale argues that the importance of this translation pattern should not be underestimated because, "In short, κεφαλή and ἀρχή, which in classical Greek have nothing in common, in biblical Greek have become closely associated by reason of their common connection with *rōsh*."[30]

The text of Is. 9.14-15 is the only example of the synonymous function of these two terms in the Greek Scriptures. This statistical information cautions the interpreter against concluding that therefore every use of κεφαλή carries with it the notion of ἀρχή (understood as "source").[31] We have already seen that the term can have the meaning of "leader" or "overlord" in addition to "beginning" or "source" (as in ἀρχή). Nevertheless, the fact that Is. 9.14-15 represents the only Scriptural text which associates κεφαλή with ἀρχή makes their presence at Col. 1.18 all the more striking.

Two points need to be stressed. First, the wide semantic range of κεφαλή can refer to social relationships and geographical phenomena. As such it has potential for being used in a number of contexts and can develop any number of themes. If the authors of Colossians and Ephesians were in need of linguistic material with potential for developing Pauline reflection about Adam and Christ, then the term κεφαλή appears to have such potential. The idea that Eve's body is drawn from Adam — suggesting that Adam is the physical "source" of Eve's bodily

---

[30] Ibid., p. 213.
[31] Those who follow Bedale's work overestimate the impact of Is. 9.14-15 to a fault. See WAYNE GRUDEM "Appendix 1: Does *kephalē* ('head') Mean 'Source' or 'Authority Over' in Greek Literature? A Survey of 2,336 Examples," pp. 43-68 (in G. KNIGHT III, *The Role Relationship between Men and Women*, Revised Edition [Moody Press: 1985]) for numerous illustrations. Grudem's works is an insightful and, I might add, needed correction to Bedale's often cited work. First, I am in basic agreement with the author's main methodological criticisms of Bedale. Second, against Grudem, I am sceptical as to whether or not one can restrict the semantic range of κεφαλή to an *either/or* question (i.e., "authority" *or* "source"). Third, the strict separation of κεφαλή from ἀρχή in texts such as Eph. 4.15-16 and Col. 2.19 (as Grundem's analysis attempts to demonstrate) does not — in my opinion — do justice to the fact that *both terms* are applied to Christ, implying that *both meanings* of the term are relevant to him. Finally, it seems quite feasible to suggest that κεφαλή can mean "authority" *and* "source" at Eph. 4.15-16 and Col. 2.19 in light of ἐξ οὗ (Eph. 4.16; Col. 2.19), which makes clear that the κεφαλη is both the absolute authority over all *as well as* the *source* of the body's growth. My sincere thanks to Prof. D. Carson for bringing Prof. Grudem's work to my attention.

existence — appears to be compatible with the notion that Christ is the "source" of growth for the church (cf. Col. 2.19 and Eph. 4.15-16). The semantic range of κεφαλή can absorb this idea. Second, the notion of Christ's Lordship in the cosmos (Col. 1.15-20; Eph. 1.22) parallels the social idea of "chief" or "ruler" found in the Greek Scriptures.

Second, my sugestion is that, in a fashion analogous to 1 Cor. 11.2-16, the presence of κεφαλή at Col. 1.15-20 also expresses its potential for connecting Christ's role as "head of the body" to the first two chapters of Genesis. If this suggestion is correct, we shall have two Pauline sources prior to Ephesians (i.e. 1 Cor. 11.3 and Col. 1.18) which connect Christ's role as κεφαλή with allusions to the first two chapters of Genesis. From the perspective of interpreting Ephesians, we see that the two Pauline texts which link Christ to Genesis may very well have been the key factors which form part of the theological agenda which guided the expansion of the address to wives at Eph. 5.22-24.

The hymn of Col. 1.15-20 expresses the supreme position of Christ within the cosmos.[32] Our primary interest is the use of κεφαλή at v.18. However, a brief glance at the context will make clear that both the hymn and κεφαλή are definitely related to parts of Genesis.[33] At Col. 1.15 we read that Christ is εἰκὼν τοῦ θεοῦ τοῦ ἀοράτου ("image of the invisible God") and that he is πρωτότοκος πάσης κτίσεως ("first born of all creation"). Clearly Jervell, Lohse and Schweizer are correct to note that at Col. 1.15 and elsewhere (e.g., 2 Cor 4.4 [cf. 3.18]) the presence of εἰκών is not directly connected to the text of (LXX) Gen. 1.26 (where εἰκών occurs). Rather, the term is mediated through Jewish Hellenistc Wisdom traditions.[34] Even so, the hypostatisization of "Wisdom" is connected to reflections about the creation of the universe (cf. Prov. 2.19; 8.30; Ps. 103.24; Job 28.23-27, etc.). That is, even if Col. 1.15 is not a direct exegesis of Gen. 1.26, those traditions[35] underlying it are ultimately rooted in Genesis. Put another way, if at Col. 1.15 Christ replaces "Wisdom," his role is still connected to Genesis and the creation of the cosmos (cf. Col. 1.16-17). The context clearly indicates that

---

[32] There are many aspects to this hymn which are debated. See E. LOHSE, *Colossians and Philemon* (Philadelphia: Fortress Press, 1971), pp. 41-61; E. SCHWEIZER, *The Letter to the Colossians*, Trans. A. CHESTER (Minneapolis, MN: Augsburg Publishing House, 1982), pp. 55-88.

[33] WITH DAVIES, *Paul and Rabbinic Judaism*, pp. 150-152 and C.F. BURNEY, "Christ as the 'APXH of Creation (Prov. VIII 22, Col. I 15-18, Rev. III 14)," *JTS* 27 (1926):160-177. JERVELL, *Imago Dei*, pp. 50, 200, n. 107, LOHSE, *Colossians*, pp. 46-47 and SCHWEIZER, *Colossians*, p. 66 and n. 27 make it clear that Col. 1.15-20 is not an exegesis of the Hebrew or Greek recensions of Gen. 1.26.

[34] JERVELL, Ibid.; LOHSE, Ibid.; SCHWEIZER, Ibid.

[35] For examples from Philo see SCHWEIZER, Ibid., pp. 65-69 and LOHSE, Ibid., pp. 46-49.

Christ's pre-eminent status in the universe is dependent on his pre-existence (v.15b) and his agency in the creation of all things (vv.16-17), both of which are linked to creation in Genesis. Even if the intended referent is not the first Adam or Christ as the New Adam, the noun κεφαλή is associated with indirect references to Genesis mediated through Wisdom traditions.

At Col. 1.18 we read that Christ "is the head (κεφαλή) of the body the church. He is the beginning (ἀρχή), the first born from the dead...". At v.18b the relative ὅς makes clear that the resurrected person of Christ is both "head" of the "body" and the "beginning," the "first born" from the dead. Therefore his resurrected status impinges upon his role as κεφαλή. The question is, in what way?

Schweizer notes that throughout the Pauline Corpus creation and resurrection are formally connected. For example, he notes that at Rom. 4.17[36] resurrection and creation or intimately linked. At 1 Cor. 8.6 the creation of the cosmos parallels the New Creation present in believers.[37] That is, mention of Christ's resurrection touches upon the idea of New Creation. This does not necessarily mean that at Col. 1.18 Christ's role as "head of the body," the "beginning" (ἀρχή) and "first born from the dead" indicates that the author of Colossians was thinking about Christ as the New Adam.[38] However, the association of the "head/body" language with Christ's resurrection does suggest that Christ could be understood as the "first" exponent of the New Creation. While the noun κεφαλή certainly expresses Christ's role as leader of the church, it seems that his role as ἀρχή and πρωτότοκος from the dead evokes the theme of New Creation and qualifies his role as κεφαλή.

On the basis of the above, it is reasonable to conclude that if the hymn of Col. 1.15-20 does not refer to Christ as the New Adam, the association of κεφαλή with εἰκών (v.15) and ἀρχή (v.18) suggests that the "head/body" language is clearly connected with the theme of New Creation by virtue of Christ's resurrected status. This text represents yet a second instance in which the term κεφαλή is clearly connected to traditions rooted in Genesis. We can see that the semantic range of κεφαλή in such that in one text (i.e., 1 Cor. 11.2-16) it refers to Adam and Eve before the fall (i.e., Gen. 1-2) while in another Pauline text (i.e., Col. 1.18) it can refer to New Creation theology, which is a christological development rooted in themes from the first two chapters of Genesis.

---

[36] The last half of Rom. 4.17 reads, "... in the presense of the God in whom he believed, who gives life to the dead and calls into existence the things that do not exist."

[37] SCHWEIZER, Ibid., pp. 75-76.

[38] Houlden certainly thinks this is the case, see his approach to the Adam motif in his comments on Col. 1.18 (*Ephesians*, p. 171).

From the above analysis there can be no doubt that at 1 Cor. 11.3 the term κεφαλή expresses Adam speculation. The use of the κεφαλή/ σῶμα language at Col. 1.18 at least implies Adam speculation. The conceptual parallels between 1 Cor. 11.3 and Eph. 5.23a-b as well as the obvious dependence of Ephesians on Colossians with respect to the use of the "head/body" imagery sustain the argument that the language of Eph. 5.22-24 is more than likely connected to Pauline theological reflections about Adam. In what follows we shall see that the author of Ephesians has molded this kind of Pauline reflection to his own ends.

D. The Theological Function of ΚΕΦΑΛΗ in Ephesians

The key to understanding the theological function of κεφαλή in Ephesians is the text of Eph. 1.19-23. The terms κεφαλή and σῶμα are associated at 1.22-23 for the first time in the epistle. The "head/body" language is associated with Christ's resurrection (vv.19-20) and God's act of placing Christ over all things for the church (v.22). The author establishes a meaning for the language which determines the reader's literary expectations when the "head/body" language is encountered at 4.15-16 and 5.23b. In other words, the text of 1.22-23 has a functional priority in that it informs the reader of what the "head/body" association initially intends.[39]

There are other reasons why 1.19-23 is a significant parallel to 5.23b. I contend that the basic thought structure of 1.19-23 is a development of that found at 1 Cor. 15.20-28, where Paul develops the Adam/Christ typology. If a link between 1 Cor. 15.20-28 and Eph. 1.19-23 can be established, such a link provides further evidence that the conceptual structure of 1.19-23 (within which the "head/body" association is inserted), is derived from a Pauline passage which explicitly develops Adam speculation. With the Adamic nature of Eph. 1.19-23 established, we will then be able to detect the Adamic function of the "head/body" association in terms of God's gift of the New Adam to the New Eve. This function, in turn, will inform our reading of 5.23.

The starting point is Eph. 5.21-33 as a whole. In this passage the terms κεφαλή, σῶμα (v.23), ὑποτάσσω (vv.21, [22], 24) and μυστήριον

---

[39] Previous research on the meaning κεφαλή is quite unsystematic. When exegetes are concerned with the *semantic meaning* of κεφαλή, typically 4.15-16 occupies center stage. E.g., SCHLIER, *Der Brief*, p. 254; *idem*, *TDNT*, p. 680; BEDALE, "The Meaning of κεφαλή," p. 215; GNILKA, *Epheserbrief*, pp. 276-277; BARTH, *Ephesians*, p. 614. When scholars raise the the question of Christ's *function* as "head," 1.22-23 takes precedence over 4.15-16 to the point where 4.15-16 does not impinge upon the analysis of 1.22-23, e.g., MASSON, *L'Épître*, p. 211; BARTH, *Ephesians*, p. 184; CAMBIER, "Le grand mystère concernant le Christ et son Église," p. 67. It is not always clear how exegetes link 1.19-23 and 4.15-16 to 5.23, see ROBINSON, *Ephesians*, p. 124.

(v.32: "mystery") occur. They also occur in the first chapter of Ephesians (κεφαλή: 1.22; σῶμα: 1.23; ὑποτάσσω: 1.22; μυστήριον: 1.9). Thus aside from the obvious parallels between 1.22-23 and 5.23 based on the "head/body" association, the vocabulary cluster of these two chapters indicates that the first chapter of Ephesians is closely related to the wife/husband relationship of 5.21-33.

When we focus on the context of Eph. 1.19-23, the importance of 1 Cor. 15.25, 27 becomes clear. Both Ps. 110.1 and Ps. 8.6 are quoted or alluded to in Eph. 1.20 (Ps. 110.1) and 22 (Ps. 8.6) and, in turn, at 1 Cor. 15.25 (Ps. 110.1) and 27 (Ps. 8.6). Except for their possible presence in 1 Pet. 3.22 and their obvious presence in the above mentioned passages, they appear together in no other New Testament texts.[40] This fact suggests that the author of Ephesians is either dependent on 1 Cor. 15.25, 27 and its immediate context, or, is drawing on a similar tradition which combined these two psalms.

It is more likely that the author of Ephesians is working with 1 Cor. 15.25, 27 or a tradition behind this text and not 1 Pet. 3.22 or Heb. 2.8. First the allusion to Ps. 8.6 is quoted verbatim in both 1 Cor. 15.27 and Eph. 1.22. Second, these two texts diverge from the Greek text of the biblical Psalm in *exactly* the same manner. Psalm 8.6 reads καὶ κατέστησας αὐτὸν ἐπὶ τὰ ἔργα τῶν χειρῶν σου· πάντα ὑπέταξας ὑποκάτω τῶν ποδῶν αὐτοῦ, while both 1 Cor. 15.27 and Eph. 1.22 read πάντα [γὰρ] ὑπέταξεν ὑπὸ τοὺς πόδας αὐτοῦ.

Third, the fact that 1 Cor. 15.25 favors the last part of Ps. 110.1 (1 Cor. 15.25: θῆ πάντας τοὺς ἐχθροὺς ὑπὸ τοὺς πόδας; Ps. 110.1: θῶ τοὺς ἐχθρούς σου ὑποπόδιον τῶν ποδῶν σου) while Eph. 1.20 favors the first part of Ps. 110.1 (Eph. 1.20: καθίσας ἐν δεξιᾷ αὐτοῦ; Ps. 110.1: κάθου ἐκ δεξιῶν μου) is not a significant challenge to my interpretation of the

---

[40] There is a wide range of opinion concerning the presence and importance of Ps. 110.1 and Ps. 8.6 in 1 Cor. 15.25, 27 and Eph. 1.20, 22. Many scholars do not recognize that both Psalms are being quoted. A minority of scholars recognize that both Pss. 110.1 and 8.6 are quoted or at least alluded to in 1 Cor. 15.25, 27 and Eph. 1.20, 22, see Lincoln, "The Use of the OT in Ephesians," p. 41; BARTH, *Ephesians*, p. 156; SCHNACKENBURG, *Der Brief*, p. 78; MASSON, *L'Épître*, pp. 154-155. Regardless of which two Psalms are identified, most scholars recognize the christological importance of them both. HOULDEN (*Ephesians*, pp. 276-277) does not comment directly on Ephesians but does point out the christological function of these psalms in independent occurrences throughout the New Testament. GNILKA (*Epheserbrief*, pp. 93-94) discusses the christological importance of Ps. 8.6 (he does not discuss the presence of Ps. 110.1 at Eph. 1.20). ABBOTT (*Ephesians*, p. 34) takes Eph. 1.22 as a "reminiscence" of Ps. 110.1 which he thinks is quoted in v.20. Both MITTON (*Ephesians*, NCB [Grand Rapids, Mich.: Eerdmans, 1981], p. 73) and SAMPLEY (*One Flesh*, p. 25, n. 2) are of the opinion that Ps. 110.1 is used twice at Eph. 1.20 and 22 and acknowledge the christological importance of its application to Christ. Others follow this opinion, see GNILKA, *Der Brief*, p. 96, n. 3 for literature. I will register my disagreement with the latter group below.

relationship between Ephesians and 1 Cor. 15. We have already seen how the author has modified the language of Col. 1.18 and 1 Cor. 11.3 at Eph. 5.23. The preference for the first part of Ps. 110.1 should be viewed in light of the author's obvious sense of freedom to modify the tradition. A. Lincoln[41] and B. Lindars[42] suggest that Paul (including Ephesians), 1 Peter and Hebrews draw on an early church tradition in their interpretations of Pss. 110.1 and 8.6. However, the close verbal contacts between 1 Cor. 15.25, 27 and Eph. 1.20, 22 are such that in this case it is not unreasonable to argue for literary dependency.

Fourth, when the use of Pss. 110.1 and 8.6 are placed alongside of the fact that in Eph. 1.22 (5.24) and 1 Cor. 15.25-28 the verb ὑποτάσσω occurs, the suggestion that 1 Cor. 15.25-28 be considered a significant source for Eph. 5.22-24 is strengthened.[43] Fifth, links between these two texts show that the conceptual or thought structure of Eph. 1.19-23 is closely related to Paul's argument in 1 Cor. 15.20-29.[44] Our interest is the apocalyptic portion of Paul's argument, vv.23-28.[45]

Paul's argument is as follows. In vv.12-19 he treats the negative implications conditional upon no resurrection (cf. v.12: εἰ δέ). In vv.20-28 Paul moves from hypothetical possibility to reality (cf. v.20: νυνὶ δέ). He treats the resurrection of Christ as an event in the past[46]

---

[41] See "The Use of the OT in Ephesians," p. 41.

[42] *New Testament Apologetics* (London: SCM Press, 1961), p. 50.

[43] I shall discuss the links between 1 Cor. 15.28 and Eph. 5.22-24 based on ὑποτάσσω below in my analysis of the church's subordination.

[44] The text of vv.20-28 can be distinguished from what precedes and follows it based on content and stylistic analysis. Commentators divide vv.12-54 on the basis of content: Barrett (*Corinthians*, pp. 346-347) attaches vv.20-33 to vv.12-19; Orr and Walker (*1 Corinthians*, pp. 346-347) as well as Robertson and Plummer (*Corinthians*, pp. 344-355) agree that vv. 20-28 ought to be distinguished as a unity, but once more on the basis of content analysis. Except for Conzelmann's solitary comment on the shift in tone and style at v.29 (*1 Corinthians*, p. 272) little has been said about stylistic matters. My suggestions on style are as follows. The stylistic homogeneity throughout vv.12-19 can be illustrated by noting that the conditional particle εἰ is combined (1) with interrogative particle (v.12: εἰ δέ ... πῶς); (2) an inferential particle (v.14: εἰ δέ ... ἄρα ... [καὶ]; v.15: ... εἴπερ ἄρα; v. 17: εἰ δέ ... , [v.18] ἄρα καὶ...), (3) a negative conjunction (v.13: εἰ δέ ... οὐδέ; v.16: εἰ γὰρ ... οὐδέ) and (4) it appears without a corresponding apodosis (v. 19: εἰ ...). In stark contrast to this stylistic feature, vv.20-28 break this pattern with νυνὶ δέ (v.20). Absent here are any conditional statements of the kind made in vv. 12-19. However, with vv.29-34, the conjunction ἐπεί introduces a number of rhetorical questions (v.29: τὶ ... τὶ; v.30: τὶ) which express a strong shift in mode and tone from that of vv.20-28 (so CONZELMANN, *Ephesians*, p. 272). The conditional particle of vv.12-19 resurfaces in a direct question at v.32 (εἰ ... τὶ), providing more stylistic links between vv.12-19 and 29-34. There can be no doubt, the text of vv.20-28 stands as an integral literary unit.

[45] On the apocalyptic character of vv.20-28 see CONZELMANN, *1 Corinthians*, p. 269 and BARRETT, *Corinthians*, p. 353.

[46] Note the use of the perfect passive ἐγήγερται at vv.4, 12 and especially at v.20.

which is the key to God's plan to reclaim the fallen cosmos. In vv.20-28 Paul explains what the resurrection means for Christ (v.20) and then for all humans (vv.21-28). That is, he links the Adam/Christ typology with death and resurrection (vv.21-22), then the role of the risen "Adam" to the resurrection of all believers at his second coming (vv.23-28).

At vv.23-28 the unfolding of God's final plan follows a definite order of events (v.23: τάγματι) which lead to the "end" (v.24: εἶτα τὸ τέλος; v.28: ὅταν ... τότε [καὶ]). When the "end" approaches, the reigning monarch[47] will once and for all destroy all hostile enemies (v.24). Coordinated with this reign is God's active role of placing all things under Christ's feet (vv.25, 27). *Once* this has been accomplished (v.25: ἄχρι), *then* (v.28: τότε) the monarch will be subordinate to God (v.28b). The end occurs within an ordered sequence of events.

The sequence of events leading to final unity with God (v.28c) suggests a cosmological hierarchy.[48] The hierarchy is structured around the allusions to Ps. 110.1 (1 Cor. 15.25) and Ps. 8.7 (1 Cor. 15.27). During Christ's reign he destroys the enemies (v.24) which God places under Christ's feet (v.25 = Ps. 110.1; v.27 = Ps. 8.7). In the second half of v.27b Paul goes to great pains to make clear that the πάντα of v.27a does not include God; God will be over all (v.28). Thus far the positioning of the characters suggests that God is over all; next is Christ; then come the enemies who are under Christ's feet. When all is accomplished, Christ will then be subordinate to God (v.28b). The picture is modified slightly by v.28c. God is over all; subordinate to God is Christ; then all things are under Christ.[49]

At Eph. 1.19-23 the author of Ephesians modifies the design of 1 Cor. 15.20-28, developing some elements while restricting others. First, with regard to structure, the "over/under" pattern of Eph. 1.21-22 reflect a cosmological hierarchy paralleling that of 1 Cor. 15.20-28. Eph. 1.21 goes to great lengths to illustrate that Christ is "far above" (ὑπεράνω) all

---

[47] Such an image is suggested by the royal terms βασιλείαν at v.24 and βασιλεύειν at v.25, as well as by the presence of Ps. 110.1 and Ps. 8.6.

[48] By "hierarchy" I do not mean the classical Aristotelian or Platonic hierarchies of being. I simply mean that there seems to be some kind of cosmological taxonomy or spatial arrangement within the cosmos. I use "hierarchy" for lack of a better term.

[49] This structure is quite similar to the one found in 1 Cor. 11.3. In both texts God is above all (1 Cor. 11.3: "the head of Christ is God"; 1 Cor. 15.24: "Christ delivers the kingship to God,"; v.28: "Christ will be subordinated [including all things put under his feet] to God"); next is Christ (1 Cor. 11.3: "the head of every man is Christ"; 15.25, 27: God puts all things under Christ's feet); then comes everything else (1 Cor. 11.3: men and women; 15.24-25: enemies and "all things"). It is interesting to note that in these two instances Paul situates Christ's cosmological import from a decidedly anthropological (1 Cor. 11.3) and soteriological (1 Cor. 15.22-28) perspective. In both instances contact with Genesis is either explicit (1 Cor. 15.21-22) or implicit (1 Cor. 11.3).

cosmological entities. At 1 Cor. 15.24 Christ's superior position over hostile cosmological entities is depicted in terms of his ability to destroy them. Eph. 1.22 emphasizes God's power to subordinate all things *under* Christ's feet (Ps. 8.7: ὑπό). At 1 Cor. 15.25 and 27 the exact same action is depicted. The result is that both texts express strikingly similar understandings of how God and the resurrected Christ relate to the cosmos. God is above all (1 Cor. 15.24, 28b-c; Eph. 1.20: Christ is raised *up to* God's right hand). Next comes Christ with all enemies under him (1 Cor. 15.25, 27; Eph. 1.21-22).

Second, at 1 Cor. 15.20-28 the final resurrection occurs in a dynamic fashion. The sequence of events and accompanying actions must take place before God can be all to everything. This sequence is dynamic and futuristic.[50] At Eph. 1.19-23 clearly the resurrection anticipated by all believers at 1 Cor. 15.20-28 seems to have been partially realized in the action of God in the believer.[51] Absent is the description of the process by which God *will* reclaim the cosmos (so 1 Cor. 15.20-28). Only the ongoing activity of God's work in the believer is reported; only God is active, Christ is totally passive. Christ does not do combat with cosmological forces. There is no mention of his subordination to the Father. The context of Eph. 1.19-23 treats the resurrection of believers (and not just of Christ) as a past event.[52] The blessings of God are already operative in the life of the believer (1.3).[53] Reading Eph. 1.19-23 in light of 1 Cor. 15.20-28 gives the reader the impression that the process described at 1 Cor. 15.20-28 is carried to its logical conclusion and then frozen still. That is, the cosmological hierarchy anticipated at the end of 1 Cor. 15.20-28 is partially realized at Eph. 1.19-23.

Clearly the structure and content of 1 Cor. 15.20-28 has been adopted and adapted at Eph. 1.19-23. This alone suggests that the image of Christ as the New Adam may be lurking in the shadows of Eph. 1.19-23. When we recall that the term κεφαλή is associated with Genesis twice in the Pauline Corpus prior to Ephesians (i.e., 1 Cor. 11.2-16 and Col. 1.15-20) and that at Eph. 1.19-23 the author clearly develops the structure and content of a text which contains a clear example of the Christ/Adam typology (i.e., 1 Cor. 15.20-28), the possibility that Eph. 1.19-23 expresses Pauline theological reflections about the New Adam is greatly enhanced.

There are two clues in Eph. 1.19-23 which tend to confirm the possibility just proposed. First, consider the use of Ps. 8.7 at 1 Cor. 15.27

---

[50] See v.22: ζωοποιηθήσονται; v.24: καταργήσῃ; v.28: ὑποταγήσεται.
[51] That the church *has already been raised with Christ* is clear from 2.6.
[52] This is quite clear with the use of aorists at v.20 (ἐνήργησεν; καθίσας) and v.22 (ὑπέταξεν; ἔδωκεν). See 2.6 as well.
[53] Cf. 1.19: the resurrection power is already in believers, cf. 2.6.

and Eph. 1.22. The psalm is a hymn of praise to God as creator (vv.3-5) and depicts "man" (ἄνθρωπος) as the highpoint of creation (vv.5-9). That this psalm is focused on the first two chapters of Genesis no one disputes. The early church saw its christological potential.[54] The application of this psalm to Christ in the context of 1 Cor. 15.20-28 suggests the idea that Christ is the New Adam. Even though this idea is not explicit in the text, the contrasts Paul draws between Adam and Christ at vv.20-21 support this reading of Ps. 8.6 at 1 Cor. 15.27. It is the structure and content of 1 Cor. 15.20-28 found at Eph. 1.19-23 and the presence of Ps. 8.6 at 1 Cor. 15.27 and Eph. 1.20 which suggest the image of Christ as the New Adam at Eph. 1.22.

Second, connections between Christ and Genesis at Eph. 1.19-23 need not be based solely on comparisons between Pauline texts. At 1.22 we note that God "gave" (ἔδωκεν) Christ as "head" to the church.[55] Barth's analysis represents one of the few attempts to account for the verb. He notes that the Hebrew verb "to give" (nātan) can sometimes means "to appoint" or "to install".[56] From this understanding of δίδωμι he then speculates that at Eph. 4.11 and probably 1.22 the notion of "to appoint" may refer to the gift character of Christ to the church, which she accepts along with the monarchical hierarchy implied in the "head/body" language.[57] Barth's insight may be correct, but the basic problem is his method of argument. By the late first century A.D. it is more likely that a Greek version of the Scriptures would have been more familiar to Christians (even of Jewish origins) than would the Hebrew version[58].

The use of δίδωμι in the Greek scriptures indicates that this verb was used at critical points in the sacred history of Israel. For example, at Gen. 9.2 God makes an important promise to Noah and his sons. God will "place" all the animal kingdom under their hands or in their control (ὑπὸ χεῖρας ὑμῖν δέδωκα). At v.12 we learn that the rainbow in the sky is a sign of the covenant which God "gives" (δίδωμι) to Noah. The very same action characterizes covenantal action between God and Abram at 12.7. God will "give" (δώσω) the land to Abram.[59] The use of δίδωμι to

---

[54] Whether "early church" refers to a pre-Pauline tradition which connected Ps. 110.1 to Ps. 8.6 or whether Paul himself made the connection is neither relevant nor pertinent to the discussion at hand.

[55] Discussion of δίδωμι at 1.22 is almost non-existent because of past pre-occupation with the intellectual background to Ephesians.

[56] He lists 1 Sam. 8.5-6; Lev. 17.11; Num. 14.4. See *Ephesians*, p. 158.

[57] *Ephesians*, p. 158.

[58] GNILKA (*Epheserbrief*, p. 97) argues that the use of δίδωμι at 1.22 is not derived from Hebrew but represents a Greek form of conceptualization.

[59] There are many other illustrations of this use of δίδωμι, see esp. (LXX) Gen. 13.15 and 15.18.

express divine activity in connection with covenantal narratives indicates the theological significance this verb has within the Greek Scriptures.

In light of the above, it is significant that δίδωμι appears at Gen. 1.29, where God gives the plants and other such food to Adam and Eve in the garden. Although there is no explicit covenantal theology expressed, God does provide Adam and Eve with life-sustaining gifts. The giving of Christ to the church at Eph. 1.22 may be an indirect allusion to Gen. 1.29.[60] In other words, the presence of this verb may in fact represent yet another aspect of the theological agenda guiding the use of the "head/body" imagery. It also emphasizes the donative character of Christ's headship for the church.[61]

In summary, the suggestion that at Eph. 1.19-23 Christ should be viewed as the New Adam of the New Creation is based on the following cumulative argument. The striking points of contact between 1 Cor. 15.20-28 and Eph. 1.19-23 are (1) the way in which God and the resurrected Christ relate to the hierarchically conceived interpretation of the cosmos; (2) the treatment of resurrection in both texts, suggesting New Creation motifs; (3) the presence of Pss. 110.1 and 8.7 in both texts, Ps. 8.7 suggesting the image of Christ as the New Adam; (4) by the exaltation of Christ in both texts: all of the central elements in the text of 1 Cor. 15.20-28 — where the Christ/Adam typology is explicit — are present at Eph. 1.19-23, further reinforcing the image of Christ as the New Adam. Second, the use of δίδωμι at 1.22 evokes the gifts God gave to Adam and Eve (and to others), suggesting yet another link back to Genesis. Third, we have already seen from my analysis of Eph. 2.14-16 that Christ's role as "head" includes his function as the eschatological Adam of the New Creation who shares in the divine act of creating.

Let me point out the role which the semantic range of κεφαλή plays in developing Pauline theological reflections about Adam in Ephesians. First, we should remember that the term is twice connected to Pauline theological reflections about Christ as the New Adam at 1 Cor. 11.2-16 and Col. 1.15-20, thus illustrating the potential of this term for expressing a wide variety of theological motifs. Second, it comes as no surprise

---

[60] KŌSHI USAMI (*Somatic Comprehension of Unity: The Church in Ephesus* An Bib 101 [Rome: Pontifical Biblical Institute Press, 1983], pp. 128-129) is correct to point out that ἔδωκεν at 1.22b is in parallel construction with ὑπέταξεν at 1.22a, which helps distinguish between Christ's *rule* over cosmological forces and the role he is given by God as κεφαλή over all *for the church*. Moreover, he is correct to point out (Ibid., p. 129, n. 220) that in Ephesians δίδωμι denotes primarily an act of God: (1) 1.17: God gives revelation and knowledge; (2) 3.2, 7-8: the grace to be an apostle and to preach the word (6.19); (3) 4.7-8, 11 God also gives gifts in/through Christ.

[61] The gift character of δίδωμι is commonplace in the undisputed letters of Paul, see Rom. 5.5; 12.3, 5; compare Rom. 15.15 with 1 Cor. 1.4. Also, recall that the Adamic nature of κεφαλή has already been established at 5.23a-b.

to note that in Ephesians this term is connected to Christ's resurrection status, thus expressing New Creation theology at 1.19-23. Certainly Christ's pre-eminent position in the cosmos is stressed. But his pre-eminent position here is based on the action of God and on his status as the *Endzeit* or eschatological "Adam" of the New Creation, as 2.14-16 makes clear. That is, Christ is "head" of the New Creation; he is first in the new series called "New Creation". Third, the "head/body" image facilitates a development of the New Creation theology. The application of this image to both Christ *and* the church indicates that the church also participates in the New Creation: is the second exponent of the New Creation. The church, who is called his "body" (1.23; 4.16; 5.23c, 30), is raised up with him in the heavenly places (2.6), is co-created by God and Christ (2.10, 15-16). All of these aspects of the church's existence, coupled with her subordination to the "head" (5.24a) from whom she draws new life and growth (4.15-16), make her the *Endzeit* or eschatological counter to the New Adam. She is the New Eve.

It should be evident that the author of Ephesians is a masterful theologian, weaving a number of Pauline themes into the fabric of a New Creation theology based in Pauline theological reflections about the eschatological Adam. In addition, it should also be clear that the theological agenda I contend is shaping the address to wives is not peculiar to Eph. 5.22-33. With the above in mind, I want to illustrate the importance 1.19-23 has for the interpretation of 5.22-24.

Let me focus this discussion by rephrasing a question asked earlier in this study. Why does the author of Ephesians qualify Christology with soteriology at Eph. 5.23b-c? That is, why is Christ's role as "head" (v.23b) qualified by his role as "savior" (v.23c)? The key to understanding this peculiar association lies in the active and passive aspects of Christ's relationship to the church and God.

As noted above, at Eph. 1.19-23 the Second Adam does not combat enemies (as he does at 1 Cor. 15.24).[62] There is no mention of the New Adam's subordination to God (1 Cor. 15.28b) nor of God's headship over Christ (1 Cor. 11.3). In Eph. 1.19-23 Christ is totally passive. He does not assume the role of "head"; it is given to him by God, who raised him up, who seated him at the right hand, who placed all things under his feet and who gave Christ as "head" over all things for the church. Christ's position as "head" is entirely an act of God.[63] Christ's role as "head" is fundamentally theological, it represents an action of God.

In light of the above, the statement "just as Christ is head of the

---

[62] Below I argue that this role has been transferred to the church.

[63] My speculation is that the headship of Christ (1.22) over the church (1.22b-23a) is the means by which God communicates his resurrection power mentioned in v.19a.

church" (5.23b) should be taken as a statement about God's divine activity, his gift of Christ to the church. According to the context of 1.19-23, the character of Christ's headship should be understood in the resurrection power which God communicates to the believer. According to 4.15-16, this gift of Christ's headship to the church also includes the understanding that Christ is the calibrator or standard of measure for the church's growth in and towards the resurrected Christ.

Recall that in the previous chapter I argued that Christ's role as "savior of the body" (5.23c) is fundamentally a reference to his death on the cross, expressed at 5.25 and 2.14-16. That is, Christ saves by dying for and, so loving, the church. Here Christ is neither passive nor instrumental. He expresses the main action. As savior of the body Christ is quite active.

When we read 5.23b-c in light of 1.19-23 and 2.14-16, the following interpretation results. The appositional phrase "he, savior of the body" (v.23c) must be viewed as Christ's active role in his relationship to the church. The action of saving includes his saving/creating the body (2.14-18). This part of the verse expresses the New Adam's role as co-creator and also savior of the New Creation. The headship of Christ, expressed at v.23b expresses a theological statement, Christ's headship over the church is God's gift of resurrection life to the church. That is, 5.23b and c coordinate the actions of God and of Christ and signal the reader that the question of headship and subordination have to do with the emerging New Creation.

The very language used to justify the subordination of the wife is dependent on New Creation theology which situates the Christ/church and wife/husband relationship within two creative and divine actions: Christ's saving action and God's creative gift to the church. Thus far it should be clear that the address to wives is imbued with Adamic motifs. Is this the case with the verb ὑποτάσσω?

E. The Subordination of the Church

According to v.24, the subordination of the church is the model for the wife's subordination. Unfortunately, discussion of the church's impact on the wife's subordination is almost non-existent. Many scholars do not even treat the church's subordination.[64] Barth's survey of the active, middle and passive forms of the verb ὑποτάσσω is useful for distinguishing between the coerced subordination of hostile cosmological

---

[64] To the following could be added many other examples, see HOULDEN, *Ephesians*, pp. 332-333; SAMPLEY, *One Flesh*, pp. 10, 27, 97, 99, 102, 108, 110, 114, 116, 118, 121, 126; ABBOTT, *Ephesians*, p. 167.

powers to God and the freely chosen subordination of Christ and the church to God.[65] The essential characteristic operative in the subordination of the latter group centers on a willingness to cooperate with the divine plan of salvation. Concrete examples which illustrate the church's subordination to Christ are the church's (1) faith, (2) confession, (3) hope, (4) and so on.[66] Scholars do not connect the church's subordination to Adamic christological reflection.[67] The above analysis of κεφαλή suggests that more can be said about the church's subordination.

My contention is that the subordination of the church at Eph. 5.24a is derived from 1 Cor. 15.28b. This derivation can be best perceived by examining how a number of "theological roles" have been transferred to the church, all of which, I contend, make clear her distinctive participation in the New Creation.

1. Theological Transfers

Let me first state that the transfer of Christ's role of subordination to the church at 5.24a is not an isolated phenomenon or a peculiar feature unique to that verse. Rather, this pattern of "theological transfer" represents a broad conceptual pattern discernible elsewhere in Ephesians. Second, recall that two of Christ's roles at 1 Cor. 15.20-28 were seen to be absent at Eph. 1.19-23.[68] It what follows, I shall account for these roles in terms of the church's participation in the New Creation.

In Pauline letters prior to Ephesians, it is not unusual to note Christ's instrumental role as co-creator of the first creation. At Col. 1.16 the RSV reads: "for in him all things were created, in heaven and on earth, visible and invisible, whether thrones or dominions or principalities or authorities — all things were created through him and for him." Christ's creative role is instrumental. He is the means by which God creates the cosmos (cf. John 1.3).

A similar role is given to Christ at 1 Cor. 8.6. The RSV reads: "yet for us there is one God, the Father, from whom are all things and for whom we exist, and one Lord, Jesus Christ, through whom are all things and through whom we exist." Christ is instrumental in the original

---

[65] *Ephesians*, pp. 708-710.

[66] Ibid., p. 619.

[67] CAMBIER, ("Le grand mystère concernant le Christ et son Église," pp. 64-65) suggests that the injunction for subordination is no doubt based on the first three chapters of Genesis, which is then completed or fulfilled in Christianity, e.g., 1 Cor. 3.23; 11.3. Cambier's work comes closest to Adamic christological reflection which is, at best, underdeveloped.

[68] I.e., His role as fighter of hostile cosmological powers (1 Cor. 15.24-25) and his role as the subordinate son (v.28b).

creation of the cosmos. That is, in both texts his role as co-creator is instrumental, one which assists God in the act of creating. Clearly God is the principle and Christ is the operative.

Christ functions in a similar fashion in the New Creation. His role is also instrumental. All who are "in Christ" are a part of the New Creation (2 Cor. 5.17), but ultimately God is the author of the New Creation (cf. 1 Cor. 1.20). The context of Col. 2.8-15 is a good illustration of the posture just described. In this text we see that the New Creation comes about in and through Christ, yet clearly it is God who does the creating. God "circumcised" believers *by* the circumcision of Christ (v.11),[69] God buries believers with Christ in baptism (v.12) and raises them with Christ (v.12). It is God who makes believers alive with Christ (v. 13: σὺν αὐτῷ). The action of God is central, the function of Christ is instrumental.

At Eph. 2.15-16 Christ's relationship to the New Creation is modified significantly. Here it is Christ who actually creates (v. 15b: κτίζω) the "one new anthropos." Verse 15 represents the first instance in which Christ is the subject of a verb which otherwise refers only to God. Even though God is still the ultimate author of creation (cf. 2.10), Christ is not restricted to his pre-existent and instrumental role as we find it in 1 Cor. 8.6 and Col. 1.16. Rather, in Ephesians, the New Adam is given a direct and active role in creating the New Eve, by means of his saving death (2.15-16).[70] What in Pauline letters prior to Ephesians was a passive-creative role becomes in Ephesians an active-creative role. This transfer of active-creative power to Christ is what I would call, for lack of a better term, a theological transfer.[71]

A similar pattern is operative within the Christ/church relationship.

---

[69] Note the instrumental function of the dative ἐν τῇ περιτομῇ of v. 11.

[70] The transfer of direct creative powers to Christ may not be the only theological transfer within the God/Christ relationship. If we read Eph. 1.10 in light of 1 Cor. 15.20-28, for which some justification has already been given, then the ultimate goal of the salvation process is seen to shift from the theocentric perspective of 1 Cor. 15.28c to a christocentric pespective at Eph. 1.10. At 1 Cor. 15.28c, God's absolute reign over all things ([τὰ] πάντα) is the end point of a process which completes his plan of salvation. According to Eph. 1.10, the goal of salvation is that all things (τὰ πάντα) be summed up in Christ. Has the concern for the finality of τὰ πάντα shifted from God to Christ? My speculation is that an affirmative answer is not impossible.

[71] Many commentators do not even discuss this role; few note Christ's new role. ABBOTT (*Ephesians*, p. 65) comments on the masculine character of καινὸν ἄνθρωπον, he does not discuss κτίζω at all. HOULDEN (*Ephesians*, p. 291) sees a parallel between Eph. 2.15 (κτίζω) and the creation of Adam at Gen. 1.26. He does not Christ's new creative role. MASSON (*L'Épître*, p. 166, n. 4) notes that in the New Testament κτίζω always has God as its subject. He is not surprised to find Christ as the subject at Eph. 2.15 because "Commes les versets 14-16 présentent l'œuvre de la rédemption du Christ, il n'est pas étonnant qu'il y soit sujet même du verbe *créer*." BARTH (*Ephesians*, p. 308) explains that Christ's creative role is not in competition with God, it is "an execution of God's decision." No one accounts for the theological transfer.

The following examples illustrate that the transfer of Christ's subordination to the church is not an isolated instance. Rather, it is but one illustration of several instances. The theological transfer within the God/Christ relationship just outlined parallels a christological transfer within the Christ/church relationship and it parallels a pneumatological transfer within the Spirit/church relationship. Below I shall argue that the author of Ephesians interpreted the subordination of Christ at 1 Cor. 15.20-28 as an essential element in the saving process which ultimately reunites the whole cosmos to God and that he transferred this christological role (1 Cor. 15.28b) to the church at Eph. 5.24a. All of this is by way of supporting the thesis that the church's subordination is ultimately soteriological and christological and is grounded in Pauline theological reflections about the Eschatological Adam. The analysis of ὑποτάσσω represents the final shred of evidence that the theological agenda guiding the expansion of the address to wives is rooted in Pauline Adam speculation.

At Eph. 1.19-23 Christ does not destroy or in any way engage in direct combat with hostile cosmological powers. Such is not the case with 1 Cor. 15.24. Christ will hand over the kingdom or rule (βασιλείαν) when or after (ὅταν) Christ has "annihilated" (καταργήσῃ)[72] all rule (πᾶσαν ἀρχὴν), all authority (πᾶσαν ἐξουσίαν) and power (δύναμιν). Christ is quite active, he annihilates, he hands over, and he subordinates himself. Christ does not battle the cosmological forces at Eph. 1.20-22; nor, as we have seen, is Christ active. Only God acts. Christ's role as warrior is conspicuously absent. Why is Christ passive? What happened to his warrior function?

At Eph. 6.10-20 the church's mandate to fight the cosmological forces of darkness is striking since such a mandate is never explicitly given to the collective and universal church prior to Ephesians.[73] The text exhorts the church to "be strong in the Lord" (v.10). Believers are to withstand the onslaughts of the devil (v.11: τοῦ διαβόλου). That is, the church is exhorted to "fight" against the powers of darkness.[74] This fight is not with blood and flesh but with cosmological entities hostile to God and is located in the heavenly places, precisely where the church has been put by God (2.5-6). This battle with cosmological forces resembles the role Christ plays in 1 Cor. 15.24-25. There he conquers enemies and destroys death.

---

[72] CONZELMANN (1 Corinthians, p. 271) translates καταργήσῃ as "annihilation."

[73] That the author of Ephesians addresses the universal church is commonplace and need not be documented here.

[74] The term ἡ πάλη occurs only at Eph. 6.12 in the New Testament. It literally means to "wrestle" with an opponent. In this case the context suggests a fight of cosmological and metaphysical proportions.

My suggestion is that Christ's fight with hostile cosmological forces is transferred to the New Eve. As one who experiences the same resurrection power operative within Christ (1.19-20), as one whose life is totally derived from and supported by the New Adam (2.15-16; 4.15-16), and, as one who is united as "one flesh" to him (5.31-32), it is the New Eve who must realize the resurrection power of God by doing battle against hostile cosmological forces by means of the organic links between the church and Christ (as "head" to "body": 1.22-23; 4.15-16; 5.23b-c; as "one flesh": 5.31-32). Because of these links, the New Eve now assumes a christological role which, prior to Ephesians, was restricted to Christ. The mandate to fight the diabolical by means of ethical behavior (6.18; 4.2-3; 5.3-4, 15-21) concretizes the manner in which the church manifests the characteristics of the New Adam of 1 Cor. 15.24-25.[75] The earthly life of the New Eve makes concrete the reality which fully exists in the heavenly places.

Another theological transfer concerns the revelation of God's wisdom, the mystery of his salvation plan for the world at Eph. 3.10. In 1 Cor. 2.6-13 Paul makes his case for the origins and authority behind the gospel he preaches. He emphasizes that the gospel he preaches is not based on the wisdom of men but rests on the power of God (v.5). The "wisdom" (about salvation) comes from God who reveals it by the Spirit. In vv. 10-13 Paul develops precisely how the Spirit actually reveals God's wisdom, his plan of salvation. God reveals this wisdom about salvation through the Spirit (v.10), who searches even the depths of God and of humans (v.11). Clearly the Spirit is the agent by which God reveals his power and his saving action.

This revelation role is transferred to the church in Ephesians. The church not only does combat with the powers (cf. 6.10), it also reveals to them the cosmic plan of God's wisdom (3.10). The wisdom of God, which could not be known by the rulers of this age, which is revealed by the Spirit[76] is, in Ephesians, revealed to the principalities and powers in the heavenly places *through the church* (Eph. 3.10: διὰ τῆς ἐκκλησίας). The church now becomes revealer. The pneumatological function of revealer is transferred to the church, the body of Christ. In this context it is not surprising to note the author's wish that the church deepen its knowledge of God, who gives believers a spirit of wisdom and of revelation (1.17)!

Why the theological transfers? Primarily because the author wishes to associate the church with the image of Christ as the New Adam, thus

---

[75] This point is made with particular force by R. WILD, "The Warrior and the Prisoner: Some Reflections on Ephesians 6:10-20," *CBQ* 46 (1984):284-298.

[76] E.g., 1 Cor. 2.8, 10, 12.

making her the New Eve of the New Creation. In this way *both* the New Adam and Eve share in God's plan of salvation. The interpretation of the "head/body" relationship in terms of the *Urzeit/Endzeit* pattern, makes this clear.

Within *Urzeit/Endzeit* interpretations of sacred history Adam becomes the eschatological model for redeemed humanity. At 1 Cor. 15.20-28 Christ is contrasted to the first Adam and becomes the New Adam, and, the new model for *Endzeit* existence, or for redeemed humanity. According to Eph. 2.15-16 redeemed humanity begins with Christ, includes the church and is expressed as the "one new anthropos." The church's existence stems from the saving and creative work of the New Adam's death on the cross (2.15-16). The "redeemed humanity" (i.e., the "one new anthropos") is linked to the New Adam as a "body" to its "head." According to 4.15-16, the New Adam is more than simply a "model" for "redeemed humanity," the church. First, the church shares in the same kind of life as the New Adam, resurrection life (cf. 1.19-20; 2.5-6). Second, the New Adam provides the measure or standard for the New Eve's growth. According to 4.15 the church is to grow into the fullness of Christ (4.13: εἰς μέτρον ἡλικίας τοῦ πληρώματος τοῦ Χριστοῦ), the mature man (4.13: ἄνδρα τέλειον). That is, the New Eve is not only dependent on the New Adam for growth, the life she draws from him must manifest the very characteristics of that life.

In other words, the church's mandate to fight cosmological battles not only stems from the organic links between the church and Christ — suggested by the "head/body" and "one flesh" images. Her mandate also stems from the very nature of the life God gives through Christ. That life must manifest eschatological characteristics of the New Adam, her model, source of life and growth. Within such a context it comes as no surprise to find Christ's cosmological battle with the powers (1 Cor. 15.20-28) transferred to the church (Eph. 6.10-20) because she has been raised with Christ (2.6), empowered to reveal God's plan of salvation (3.10) within a lifestyle which constantly seeks to know the will of God and to live it empowered by the filling of the Spirit (5.17-21).

2. The Subordination of the Church

The church's subordination (Eph. 5.24a) represents yet another theological transfer. Once more reference to 1 Cor. 15.20-28 and Adam speculation proves illuminating. Above I argued for the relevance of 1 Cor. 15.20-28 in the interpretation of κεφαλή at Eph. 1.22 and 5.23b. The text of 1 Cor. 15.27-28 can shed great light on understanding the theological nature of the church's subordination.

The text of 1 Cor. 15.21-22 makes clear Christ's role as the Second Adam of the New Creation. At vv.20-28 Christ plays an active role in bringing about the final reconciliation between the cosmos and God. He annihilates cosmological forces hostile to God and he hands over the kingdom to God. Finally, when all is accomplished, then the son will subordinate himself to the Father (v.28b). At Eph. 1.19-23 Christ is quite passive. There is no mention of Christ's subordination to the Father. What happened to this role?

The text of 1 Cor. 15.20-28 makes it quite clear that the subordination of the son to God brings to completion a plan in which God is reconciled to all. Then son will subordinate himself *so that* (v.28c: ἵνα) God can be all to everything (v.28c: ἵνα ᾖ ὁ θεὸς τὰ πάντα ἐν πᾶσιν). The subordination of Christ to God is the last step (cf. v.24: εἶτα τὸ τέλος) of a process (cf. vv.24-28) whereby God finally reconciles the cosmos to himself. According to 1 Cor. 15.20-28, subordination is essential to Paul's view of how the final plan of salvation will occur at the *parousia* or second coming.

This text is relevant to the subordination of the church (Eph. 5.24a) for the following reasons. First, like Christ in 1 Cor. 15.20-28, the church is given a *cosmological* role in Ephesians. She has been raised up with Christ "in the heavenly places" (2.6) where she has been blessed with all spiritual blessings (1.3). Second, like Christ in 1 Cor. 15.20-28 and the Spirit (1 Cor. 2.8, 10, 12), the church plays a key role vis-à-vis God's plan of salvation. The church reveals that plan to the cosmological powers in the heavenly places (3.10) and does combat with the forces of the devil (6.12). That is, in Ephesians the church is an important agent effecting the unity of (literally) everything with Christ (1.10).

The above analysis confirms the contention that the subordination of the son at 1 Cor. 15.28, absent at Eph. 1.19-23, is transferred to the church at Eph. 5.24a. Not only are Pss. 110.1 and 8.6 imported from 1 Cor. 15.25, 27 at Eph. 1.20, 22, so are the theme of resurrection and the hierarchically structured picture of the cosmos. We can best account for the absence of the son's subordination at Eph. 1.19-23 by first noting that the presence of the verb would complicate the task of understanding Christ's role as κεφαλή. The author would be forced to explain how the κεφαλή is over all things yet subordinate to God as well. Second, the presence of the verb in vv.19-20 would be out of context since it would represent the only activity of Christ in a passage where he is absolutely passive. Third, mention of the son's subordination would distract the reader from the focus of the passage, God's works of resurrection power in the believer's life. Clearly the application of the son's subordination would not fit the context of 1.19-23.

The relocation of Christ's subordination in the Christ/church relationship at 5.24a is understandable given the nature of that relationship. Christ's relationship to the church involves salvation. He saves the body (5.23c) by loving it and dying for it (5.25b-27), by initially creating it

(2.15-16) and by maintaining its resurrected life and its growth (4.15-16). All of these activities are salvific and contribute towards the unity between Christ and the church. Within such a context, the subordination of the church to Christ (Eph. 5.24a), like that of Christ to God (1 Cor. 15.28b), must be understood as a critical element in the salvific plan of uniting all things to God (1 Cor. 15.28c) or to Christ (Eph. 1.10). In the context of Ephesians, the church's subordination to Christ represents an initial realization of Eph. 1.10. That is, the unification of all things in Christ begins with the Christ/church relationship, with the church's subordination to Christ. They are "one flesh" (Eph. 5.31) in this soteriological sense.[77]

3. The Church: the New Eve

The new roles attributed to the New Eve are most striking when situated within the historical context of Jewish Adam/Eve traditions in the intertestamental period. Within this literature Eve is constantly portrayed as the "weaker sex," the true reason for the existence of sin. She, and not Adam, is responsible for sin-induced-suffering. It is her gullibility and her inability to avoid falling victim to the deceiver that characterizes her "weaker" position in relation to Adam.

A good example of Eve's aptitude for deception can be found in *Vita Adae et Evae* 9.1-5. After 18 days of penance in the bone chilling waters of the Tigris, Eve is deceived by Satan. He appears in the form of an angel of brightness, luring her out of the water and therefore out of her penance. It is interesting to note Adam's reaction to seeing Eve with Satan, at 10.3-4 we read: "O Eve, Eve, where is the work of your penitence? How have you *again* been seduced by our enemy, ..." [emphasis added][78] If anyone is going to be deceived time and time *again*, it will be Eve.

Another example is 2 Enoch 30.17-18. Eve is called "mother," but she is actually bringer of death. Such an attribute comes from the lips of God himself. The texts reads: "And I assigned a shade for him; and I

---

[77] Other sources which could account for the subordination of the church can be ruled out for various reasons. The subordination of the wife at Eph. 5.22 cannot be considered because of the ellipsis of the verb. The subordination of the wife at 1 Cor. 14.34 and Col. 3.18 should be eliminated since these texts treat subordination from a strictly domestic point of view (i.e., the earthly level). Given the cosmological and soteriological role of the church throughout Ephesians, we can best account for the subordination of the church if we think of this in terms of a transfer of christological function from Christ (1 Cor. 15.28b) to the church.

[78] See J.H. CHARLESWORTH, General Editor, *The Old Testament Pseudepigrapha*, 2 vols. (Garden City, New York, 1984-1985), vol. 2, *Expansion of the "Old Testament"*, p. 260. All translations are from Charlesworth unless otherwise indicated.

imposed sleep upon him and he fell asleep. And I took from him a rib. And I created him a wife, so that death might come to him by his wife. And I took his last word, and I called her name Mother, that is to say, Euva."[79] Here we have the image of "bringer of death" rather than "giver of life."

A similar notion is expressed in the so-called "Apoc. Mos." 7.1,[80] where Adam explains that his very death is caused by Eve. In response to Seth's question about the nature and origins of death Adam responds, "When God made us, me and your mother, *through whom I am dying*, He gave us every plant in Paradise. but concerning one he commanded us not to eat of it, for we would die of it..." [emphasis added][81] That is, Adam dies *because* of Eve's sin.

In Sir. 23.23 a similar idea of Eve is expressed somewhat differently. The three reasons for the existence of sin and death have their origins in "woman" (i.e., Eve, see also 1 Enoch 69.6). The RSV of Sir. 23.23 reads: "For first of all, she has disobeyed the law of the Most High; second, she has committed offense against her husband; and third, she has committed adultery through harlotry and brought forth children by another man."[82]

The perception of Eve as the initiator of sin and death — without any reference to Adam's responsibility — escalates to remarkable heights. In Apoc. Mos., Eve not only accepts her culpability for the fall, but because of this acceptance, she is pictured as one who should therefore desire to carry Adam's burden in the hope that God might let *Adam* (and *not* Eve) return to the garden (cf. 9.2, 10.26 11.1-3). At Apoc. Mos. 21.3, the scenario depicts Eve as Adam's seductress, with the devil himself speaking through her very mouth. Eve is deceived by Satan who speaks through the mouth of the serpent. She not only agrees to eat the fruit from the Tree of Life, she also agrees to give the fruit to Adam. After she eats the fruit, she becomes aware of her travail, is convinced to keep her oath to deliver her husband and narrates the following to her children, "For when he came, I opened my mouth *and*

---

[79] See CHARLESWORTH, *Pseudepigrapha*, vol. 1, p. 152.

[80] The title "Apocaplypse Moses" is taken as a reference to the Greek recension of the "Life of Adam and Eve." For a discussion of these and related problems see J.H. CHARLESWORTH, *The Pseudepigrapha and Modern Research*, SBLSBS 7 (Missoula Montana: Scholars Press, 1976), pp. 159-160.

[81] See CHARLESWORTH, *Pseudepigrapha*, vol. 2, p. 271.

[82] I readily grant that the text is speaking about "woman" in general and not about Eve in particular. However, the treatment of the woman at Sir. 23.23 is in character with the treatment of Eve at Sir. 25.21-26, and esp. at v.24, which reads, "From a woman sin had its beginning, and because of her we all die." Clearly the text from Sir. 23.23 is connected to 25.24 since both speak about women and sin. I take the text of 25.24 to be a key expression of the author's perception of how sin and women are to be connected.

the devil was speaking, and I began to admonish him [Adam] saying 'Come, my lord Adam, listen to me and eat of the fruit of the tree of which God told us not to eat from it, and you shall be as a God'." [emphasis added] Satan uses Eve as a means of getting to Adam. He even speaks through Eve as he did through the serpent. Eve and the serpent are twin instruments in the Satanic ploy against humanity.

A final example brings us to what I take to be the epitomy of the treatment of Eve. At *Vita Adae et Evae* 2.2-3.2 we read: "And Adam rose and walked seven days over all that land, and found no food such as they had had in paradise. And Eve said to Adam: 'Would you kill me? O that I would die! Then perhaps the Lord God will bring you into paradise, for *it is because of me* that that the Lord God is angry with you'." [emphasis added] That is, Eve wishes Adam to *kill* her for her part in the fall (cf. 19.2: 11.1-3). Adam refuses, for he cannot see himself putting forth his hand on "his own flesh" (3.2). However, in the Greek Apoc. Mos. Adam is less genteel. He confesses his desire to kill Eve (for causing their expulsion from the garden), but refrains from this *only* because he fears destroying the image which God created in Eve (cf. 29.7-11).[83]

This perception of Eve has found its way into parts of the New Testament. For example, in 1 Tim. 2.14, the question of the order of being (v.13: "for Adam was first, them Eve") surfaces in an argument illustrating why Eve — and not Adam — was deceived. Such an argument then serves to address the behavior of married women (v.14). The question of the woman being especially vulnerable to Satanic deception is applied to the local Corinthian church, again with reference to Eve (cf. 2 Cor. 11.2-3). The sinful, gullible and certainly "weaker" Eve is paraded as an "example" to be avoided. It is Eve and *not* Adam who seems to bear full responsibility for occasioning sin and death into the world.

If the first Eve was disobedient to God's commands, the source of Adam's decline and death and the "weak link" in the human chain by which all humans would suffer and die, then the New Eve of Ephesians is the obedient and subordinate helpmate of the New Adam. Together with God they bring about the New Creation. Unlike the first Eve, not only is the New Eve not vulnerable to deception and not defenseless against the lures of Satan, she actually does battle with Satan (Eph. 6.12) and

---

[83] I have not treated Rabbinic examples because of the problem with dating the texts. Scroggs reports many commentators agree that the Rabbinic understanding of Eve's sin concerns her having intercourse with the Serpent/Satan figure. In other words, the depictions of Eve in Rabbinic literature are quite similar to those in the Pseudepigraphical literature. See SCROGGS, *The Last Adam*, p. 74, n. 4.

reveals to his cohorts the wisdom of God's plan of salvation (3.10). If the first Eve had first hand responsibility in bringing about the decay and fall of humanity and creation, the New Eve reverses this pattern in that certain christological and pneumatological functions are transferred to her. The "bearer of death" has become the "bearer of life."

F. Conclusions

It should be clear that in Ephesians the language which describes the Christ/church relationship is derived from Pauline theological reflections about the eschatological or *Endzeit* Adam. How does the image of a "body" subordinate to its "head" (5.22-24) relate to the idea of the mutual "one flesh" relationship (5.31-32)?

First, within the context of Ephesians, mutuality and subordination within the Christ/church relationship must be understood in terms of the salvation process. Both aspects of the one relationship have the same goal or finality: to unite all things in Christ (1.10). The process of uniting all things in Christ is initially realized in the Christ/church relationship, expressed in the "one flesh" imagery. That this process towards salvific unity is initially realized in the church's life is clear from a number of passages. Christ is "savoir of the body" (5.23c); the church has already been raised with Christ (2.6); her very existence is derived from the New Adam's creative life giving death at the cross (2.15-16); the church's life is sustained and (4.15-16) and perfected by Christ (5.26-27). The plan to unite all things in Christ begins in the New Adam/Eve relationship. The biblical "one flesh" imagery is eschatological in the sense that it signals an initial realization of the final stage of salvation.

Second, the "head/body" and "subordination" language expresses actions which lead to the eschatological "one flesh" unity. Christ creates the New Eve, the second exponent of the New Creation (2.15-16); God gives Christ as "head" for the church (1.22); Christ sustains her (4.15-16), saves her (5.23c) and purifies her (5.26-27). But this does not mean that the church is a passive appendage to Christ. The transfer of theological roles rules out this interpretation. As the second exponent of the New Creation, the church is active, she executes salvific tasks originally proper to Christ and the Spirit.

More specifically, the church reveals God's plan of salvation to the cosmos (3.10), does battle with hostile cosmological forces (6.12) and subordinates herself to Christ (5.24a). As the second exponent of the New Creation, the New Eve assumes christological and pneumatological functions which represent her unique contributions to the saving process. The New Adam empowers and the New Eve acts; as "one flesh" they have mutual responsibilities in executing God's plan of uniting all things to Christ. Mutuality is defined by the unique roles they execute in the salvation process. In Ephesians the two foci of salvation are Christ and the church. Together they represent a complimentory effort in which all things will be united in Christ.[84].

In Ephesians, the "head/body" and "subordination" language is action language expressing the manner in which salvific unity occurs. Christ creates the church (his "body"), God gives Christ to the church (as "head"), the church is subordinate to Christ. The "one flesh" language expresses the initial realization of the salvific action expressed in the "head/body" and "subordination" language. The address to wives (5.22-24) describes in action terms what is already realized in eschatological and biblical imagery (5.31-32).

---

[84] The fact that in Ephesians the church is subordinate to Christ and not God is not as problematic as it might at first appear. Recall that Christ assumes a number of distinctively theological functions. Christ is the subject of the verb κτίζω at Eph. 2.15, not God. That is, Christ assumes a role that is, strictly speaking, theo-logical. In addition, recall that in Ephesians the goal of salvation is to unite all things in Christ and not, strictly speaking, in God (cf. 1.10). That is, the finality of the salvation process concludes with all things united in Christ. Within this scheme of theological adjustments, the subordination of the church to Christ parallels the subordination of Christ to God.

CHAPTER V

Wives and Husbands

A. Introduction

In the previous chapters I offered a number of arguments in support of my contention that both the injunction for subordination and the language used to justify it are derived from Pauline and Jewish forms of theological speculation about Adam. In this chapter I want to return to the text of Eph. 5.22-24 and interpret it in light of my contention. Then I shall draw some exegetical conclusions and offer some hermeneutical reflections.

B. Eph. 5.22-24

1. Eph. 5.22: αἱ γυναῖκες τοῖς ἰδίοις ἀνδράσιν ὡς τῷ κυρίῳ

It is nothing short of remarkable that the author of Ephesians addresses the question of the wife's subordination without applying the verb ὑποτάσσω directly to the wife! The verb occurs only at v.24a, in connection with the church. Verses 22 and 24b — where the wife is addressed directly — do not contain any verbs. In addition, the absence of any verb in connection with the behavior of Christian wives is without precedent within the New Testament as a whole.[1]

Two questions present themselves. First, why does the author avoid the verb ὑποτάσσω when addressing the wife at vv.22 and 24b? Second, why does the verb occur only in connection with the church at v. 24a? At the risk of making too much out of (literally) nothing (i.e., the ellipsis), my contention has been that the construction of the address to wives without the verb ὑποτάσσω at vv. 22, 24b is best explained as the author's attempt to redefine the wife's subordination by linking it to the subordination of the eschatological community at v.21 and v.24a. Such a link makes clear the ecclesiological nature of the wife's subordination. With this in mind we can interpret v.22 in the following manner.

The ellipsis of the verb at v.22 causes the reader to take vv.17-21 into account when interpreting the wife's subordination. This linguistic

---

[1] See Col. 3.18; 1 Tim. 2.11; Titus 2.5; 1 Pet. 3.1 and the disputed 1 Cor. 14.34.

feature represents the first illustration of how the lifestyle of individual members of the church has a direct impact on the wife's subordination. But to what effect? The eschatological nature of the wife's subordination indicates that it is part of God's intent for *Endzeit* or redeemed humanity.

The author provides some clues as to why subordination is necessary in the redeemed community: subordination is a concrete extension of what it means to do the will of the Lord (v.17) and a concrete illustration of how both the community and the wife become filled with the spirit (v.18). The church's subordination to each other (v.21) and to Christ (vv.21b, 24a) provides the wife — who is also subordinate to Christ (v.22: ὡς τῷ κυρίῳ) — with both earthly or practical (vv.17-21) and theological or ideal examples (v.24a) of subordination. Just as the members of the church are subordinate to each other in the fear of Christ (v.21), so must the wife be subordinate to the husband as to the Lord. The lifestyle of the wife's "brothers and sisters in Christ," which includes knowing the will of the Lord (v. 17) and all the activities listed in vv.18-22, represents *the* paradigm for the wife's subordination. Her subordination is not an isolated injunction but rather an intricate part of the fabric of life within the redeemed community. Her subordination, like that of the community, is a sign of knowing God's will and of being filled in the spirit.

The function of the phrase "as to the Lord" comes into sharper focus with the above in mind. Its presence at v.22 guards against a potentially harmful interpretation which could absolutize examples of subordination if understood strictly "from below." In effect, both the phrases ἐν φόβῳ Χριστοῦ (v.21: "in the fear of Christ") and ὡς τῷ κυρίῳ (v.22: "as to the Lord") remind both the community (v.21) and the wife (v.22) that the human or horizontal dimensions of subordination are ultimately qualified by subordination to Christ, thus adding a vertical and christological dimension to the earthly sphere of subordination.

My interpretation of v.22 could be paraphrased in the following manner. "Wives, be subordinate to your own husbands just as members of the community are subordinate to one another [v.21]. In this way the whole community acts in a way which expresses knowledge of the Lord's will [v.17] and the whole community pursues a life of being filled with the spirit [v.18]. This lifestyle of being filled in the spirit is what empowers both you and the members of the community to actualize the kind of subordination the church now realizes in its relationship with Christ. In this way both you and the community form part of the New Creation. But remember, the kind of subordination which the church exercises does not begin or end in the community but is ultimately rooted in a [healthy] fear and respect of the Lord [v.21]. In your case, the requirement of subordination to your husband encompasses your relationship to the Lord, which is the foundation of your relationship to your husband [v.22]."

The wife should find ample illustrations of "redeemed" subordination within the redeemed community, which includes how males relate to males and not just how women or wives relate to men and husbands. In addition, she should also find an example of "redeemed" subordination in the collective subordination of the church — the New Eve — to the Lord. Only the ecclesiological nature of the wife's subordination emerges at v. 22. The reader encounters the use of Adamic language at vv.23-24. With the ecclesiological nature of the wife's subordination clearly established at v.22, the author can now provide motivation in support of the injunction.

2. Eph. 5.23: a ὅτι ἀνήρ ἐστιν κεφαλὴ τῆς γυναικὸς
             b ὡς καὶ ὁ Χριστὸς κεφαλὴ τῆς ἐκκλησίας,
             c αὐτὸς σωτὴρ τοῦ σώματος

The ὅτι clause at v.23 introduces the headship analogy, which provides motivation for the wife's subordination. The most striking feature of the analogy is that it presents several levels of motivation for the wife's subordination. These levels of motivation are rooted in Christology, soteriology and, properly speaking, theology.

In my second chapter I argued that at v.23 the function of ὡς is deictic. That is, it implies an identity between analogues and not similarity or comparison.[2] Yet, I also pointed out the grammar of 5.23b-c suggests that v.23c ("he, savior of the body") should be taken as an appositional phrase, distinguishing between the headship of Christ and that of the husband — only Christ is "head" *and* savior. Precisely how is the headship of the husband to be identified with that of Christ if it does not include the role of saving his wife?

Two exegetical options present themselves, both of which link the headship analogy with Christ's role as savior. The first option, although not very convincing, is accepted by several scholars and therefore should be addressed.[3] The position often advanced is that the headship and savior roles apply equally to Christ as they do to the husband. The argument is based on the headship analogy between the husband and Christ. Both are "head" in an identical fashion. The deictic function of ὡς supports this interpretation at least as far as v.23a-b is concerned.

---

[2] See MURAOKA, "The use of 'ΩΣ in the Greek Bible," p. 59.
[3] For Barth's discussion of the question and a list of those who hold this position see *Ephesians*, pp. 611-613.

Because the headship analogy clearly identifies the husband's role as "head" with Christ's role as "head," and because v.23c ("he, savior of the body") elaborates Christ's headship, it is reasonable to conclude that Christ's role as "savior" also provides further definition for the husband's headship role as well.

According to this line of interpretation, the phrase "he, savior of the body" qualifies the headship of the husband through Christ or directly qualifies both forms of headship. This position must be rejected in light of the second option, which interprets 5.23c as an appositional phrase. As an appositional phrase, the antecedent for αὐτὸς at v.23c is normally the most proximate and definite (i.e., articular) noun. In this case the most proximate antecedent is the masculine singular articular ὁ Χριστὸς at v.23b. This interpretation eliminates reference to the husband altogether. In addition, at v.23 αὐτὸς is singular and can therefore have only one referent. It would have to be plural in order to refer to both the husband and Christ.[4]

The second option is preferred because it follows the grammar of the passage, which restricts the soteriological function to Christ's level of the analogy. Because the αὐτὸς of v.23c can only refer to Christ at v.23b, v.23c is taken as an appositional phrase qualifying v.23b.[5] This line of argumentation simply points out that any link between the husband and Christ is based on the headship analogy and not on the headship/savior amalgam relevant to Christ. In effect, Christ's role as "savior of the body" does not impinge upon the husband/Christ analogy, as the grammar of vv.23b-c makes clear.[6] From the above discussion it is

---

[4] For literature and cogent arguments supporting this position see Barth, *Ephesians*, pp. 615-619, 625.

[5] E. Best, (*One Body in Christ; a Study of the relationship of the Church to Christ in the Epistles of the Apostle Paul* [London: S.P.C.K., 1955], p. 174) argues that the analogy is "not perfect" because Christ's role as "savior" of the church includes the additional claim of the church's obedience; with only slight variations, others accept that the analogy between the headship of Christ and the husband is not exact, see Masson, *L'Épître*, p. 211; Abbott, *Ephesians*, p. 166; Barth, *Ephesians*, p. 613; Cambier "Le grand mystère concernant le Christ et son Église," pp. 50, 59, 62, 64-68. Others hold a position similar to my own, on different grounds. Sampley (*One Flesh*, p. 125) suggests that v.23c does limit the husband's headship by excluding the soteriological role. Yet he argues (p. 126) that the limitation of the husband's headship in not way limits the wife's subordination. In this instance, the analogy is almost deictic (against this see Barth [*Ephesians*, pp. 610-614] who argues that there are limitations to the wife's subordination precisely because of the soteriological distinction). Robinson (*Ephesians*, p. 124) observes that what applies to the Christ/church relationship applies "in a lower sense" to the husband/wife relationship. In effect, his interpretation presupposes the deictic function of ὡς at v.23b.

[6] This is not to say that v.23c is irrelevant to the wife's subordination. Christ's role as "savior" effects the wife's subordination through the agency of the church. I take the ἀλλὰ ὡς ("just as") of v. 24a not as an adversative but as a consecutive, meaning that

reasonable to conclude that the identification between the husband and Christ at v.23b (ὡς) is based on and restricted to the question of headship.[7] Therefore the question of providing motivation for subordination is primarily centered on those properties of the term "head" which relate to both Christ and the husband.

The analogical priority of the Christ/church relationship demands that we examine Christ's headship before we can understand what is intended for the husband. Three points can be stressed.

First, according to my interpretation of 1.19-23, the "head/body" imagery expresses how God creates the "head/body" unity: he gives Christ as "head" to the church, Christ's "body." Second, the application of κεφαλή to Christ expresses more than just the divinely intended unity between Christ and the church. At 5.23b-c the term is qualified by Christ's role as savior. Christ's role as savior of the body also includes his co-creative role on the cross (2.14-15). Thus the "head/body" imagery reflects the co-ordinated efforts of God and Christ. They both create the church (cf. 2.10, 14-16) and fill it with that new life (1.19; 4.15-16). That is, 5.23b-c represents two theological *foci*, the act of God who creates unity between Christ and the church and the saving action of Christ, who with God creates and saves the church.

Third, these two theological *foci* lead to the suggestion that both the terms "head" and "body" express New Creation theology. Other evidence confirms this suggestion. We have already seen that at 1 Cor. 11.2-16 and Col. 1.15-20 the application of κεφαλή to Christ is already connected to Pauline theological reflections about the eschatological Adam. The impact of 1 Cor. 11.3 on Eph. 5.23a-b and the impact of 1 Cor. 15.20-28 on Eph. 1.19-23 together suggest that at Eph. 1.19-23 and 5.23a-b Christ is to be understood as the New Adam of the New Creation. That is, the application of κεφαλή to Christ expresses not only Christ's superior position in the cosmos, it also expresses his role as the first exponent of the New Creation. The mere association of the church

---

v.24a does not represent a break in the train of thought but continues and further elucidates what is stated immediately prior to it. According to Turner (*A Grammar of New Testament Greek*, p. 330) when ἀλλά occurs before a command (as it does at Eph. 5.24a which is just before v.24b where the command for subordintion is resumed), ἀλλά can have a consecutive force. See Mk. 9.32; 16.7; Mt. 9.18; Acts 9.6; 10.20; 20.16.

[7] Parenthetically, the interpretation of v.23c taken here is preferable because it manifests a logical consistency with vv.21 and 22. Above I argued that the phrases "in the fear of Christ" (v.21) and "as to the Lord" (v.22) may represent the author's caution against understanding the question of subordination from a strictly anthropocentric point of view. At v.23c the phrase "he, savior of the body" may also be a caution against an absolute equating of the husband with Christ. If this line of thinking is correct, we can only marvel at the author's ability to maintain a rather delicate balance between the christocentric and anthropocentric tensions within the text.

with Christ — she is his "body" — suggests that she also forms part of the New Creation. The depiction of the church as having been raised with Christ (cf. 2.6) confirms this suggestion. Together they represent the New Adam and New Eve of the New Creation, the first two exponents of the New Creation. It should be clear that the "head/body" image (1) communicates God's donative action which results in an eschatological unity (2) expresses New Creation theology, resulting in the understanding that Christ and the church are the New Adam and New Eve of the New Creation and (3) that this unity expresses God's intent for redeemed humanity.

The husband/Christ (5.23a-b) and wife/church (5.24) analogies make clear that the wife and husband also participate in the "head/body" imagery — what is said of the Christ/church relationship also applies to them. But care must be taken here, since not everything that is said of Christ applies equally to the husband. For example, it is difficult — if not impossible — to argue that the husband's role as "head" is in any way analogous to Christ's cosmological supremacy, absolute rule and coercive might. These characteristics are primarily soteriological and represent the saving actions of God and Christ. Nowhere in Ephesians do we find any human assuming such roles. In addition, these saving roles cannot possibly be applied to the husband because the appositional phrase at 5.23c ("he, savior of the body") distinguishes between Christ and the husband precisely on the basis of soteriology and therefore eliminates the possibility of the husband sharing any of these functions within marriage.

The points of contact between the husband and Christ are as follows. By analogy, the husband's headship is ultimately rooted in a divine creative act which is donative in nature and which seeks to create eschatological unity. Because this unity is eschatological, it expresses God's intent for the New Creation. The theological context of the headship language establishes the critical function of the analogy, which intends to associate Christian marriage to the New Creation manifest in the New Adam/Eve relationship of Christ and the church. Ultimately, the husband's role as "head" represents a creative act of God which links him to the New Creation mediated through Christ's headship. This also means that the husband's loving headship must be modelled on that of the New Adam. The author makes clear that the object of the wife's subordination — headship of the husband — is not "from this world". Rather, it is based on the sacrificial love of the New Adam.

---

[8] The most recent booklength study of New Testament and ancient philosophical treatments of subordination is BALCH's *Let Wives be Submissive*, pp. 23-62; see also G. DELLING's work on ὑποτάσσω, *TDNT*, VIII, pp. 39-45; J. LEIPOLDT, *Die Frau in der antiken Welt und im Urchristentum*, pp. 13-49.

The motivation for subordination given at Eph. 5.23 must be understood in light of the theological agenda just outlined. The wife is exhorted to be subordinate to the husband's Christ-like and therefore other-centered love for the following reasons. First, in accepting her husband as "head," the wife recognizes and accepts that her husband's love ultimately expresses God's gift to her. Second, the husband's headship also indicates God's intent for a new kind of unity, one which has already been formed in the Christ/church relationship, expressed in the "one flesh" image at Eph. 5.31. Third, her subordination to the husband's agapic love signals their similarity to the Christ/church relationship and consequently their own unique and concrete expression of eschatological unity. Subordination to a Christ-like headship expresses the wife's participation in the New Creation. In a manner of speaking, they become "one flesh" as Christ and the church already are "one flesh" (Eph. 5.31-32).

Both the construction of the injunction for subordination at 5.21-22, 24 and the husband/Christ analogy at 5.23a-b redefine the wife's subordination. She must subordinate herself not just to her husband who is "head"; rather, she must subordinate herself to Christ's love expressed through the husband. This is not "carte blanche" for the husband. The author is quite specific about the fact that subordination is to selfless love — expressed through the husband's headship — and not to the whims of the husband.

The author goes to great lengths to make clear to wives that their subordination is of an order quite different from philosophical arguments about the order of being or social order based on gender distinction. Within the context of Eph. 5.22-24 and the epistle as a whole, subordination to a "head" belongs to the order of New Creation and has a specific point of reference — Christ's selfless and sacrificial love.

3. Eph. 5.24: a ἀλλὰ ὡς ἡ ἐκκλησία ὑποτάσσεται τω Χριστῷ
           b οὕτως καὶ αἱ γυναῖκες τοῖς ἀνδράσιν ἐν παντί

At v.24 the author not only recalls the ecclesiological nature of subordination expressed at v.22, here he makes clear that the collective subordination of the church — the New Eve — represents *the paradigm* for the wife's subordination. Reference to the subordination of the collectivity of believers (v.24) now allows the author to connect the wife's subordination to that of the New Eve.

That the author wishes to stress the church's subordination as *the paradigm* for the wife is clear from the following. First, stated negatively, the verb ὑποτάσσω does not appear when the wife is being addressed. Both the absence of the verb in a context which surely demands its presence and the abundant witness of the tradition about the subordination of wives in New Testament and elsewhere suggests that the author is clearly modifying the address to the wife.[8] The reader, whether ancient or contemporary, cannot but be struck with the absence of the verb and is forced to consider the context. The context of v.22 (i.e. vv.17-22) clearly indicates that the wife's subordination is qualified by that of the eschatological community, as argued above. As if the linguistic signal at v.22 were not enough, the reader is forced to encounter an ellipsis of the verb for a second time at v.24b. Once more the previous linguistic unit — where we read that the church is subordinate to Christ — supplies the verbal idea, as argued above. The absence of verbs at vv.22 and 24b stresses the importance of the church as the model for subordination.

Second, stated positively, the reader directly encounters the verb ὑποτάσσω only with reference to the church. The syntax of the passage and the analogies between the wife and church make the church's subordination paradigmatic for the wife. The impression is that the author of Ephesians systematically forces the reader to think analogically with respect to understanding the wife's subordination. The absence of the verb at vv.22 and 24b force the reader to immediately and momentarily shift the focus away from the wife, placing emphasis on the context of the church's subordination found at vv.17-21 and v.24a. Then, with information provided by the context, the reader must assess what is being said about the wife by means of implied analogical (vv.17-22) and explicit analogical (v.24) thinking. Clearly, the subordination of individual believers amongst themselves (vv.17-22) and their collective subordination — as the New Eve — to Christ (v.24a) highlights the paradigmatic nature of the church's subordination.[9]

If it is clear that the church's subordination to Christ is paradigmatic for the wife, it now remains to make clear its christological underpinnings and how these are related to the wife/husband relationship.

Previous approaches to defining "subordination" lead to insights that support the contention that the church's subordination is fundamentally christological. However, scholars do not always take the church's subordination into account when analyzing that of the wife. Sampley interprets the wife's subordination in terms of her being obedient to her husband in all things. The church's subordination does not play a significant role in his analysis.[10] Masson recognizes that the

---

[9] So SCHANACKENBURG (*Der Brief*, p. 252), "Das Verhalten der Frau steht durch die Einführung des Musters "Christus-Kirche" von vornherein in einer Korrelation zum Verhalten des Mannes, der nach dem Vorbild Christ seiner Frau äußerste Liebe, Sorge und Pflege angedeihen lassen soll."

[10] See *One Flesh*, p. 126. Sampley's initial position, that the mutual subordination of v. 21 may be a critique of the *Haustafel* tradition, is promising. But such promise seems to wither in light of his statement that the limitation of the husband's authority in no way

wife's subordination is no doubt voluntary, but is none the less absolute
and complete. It is her loving response to the love of her husband.[11]
Schnackenburg takes a similar approach. He recognizes that the verb
ὑποτάσσω prompts the notion of order within a distinctive social
structure which understands ὑποτάσσω in term of a presumed duty.[12] He
resists the interpretation that such a presumed duty is necessarily legal in
Ephesians. Rather, the analogy between the wife and the church
suggests that the wife's subordination is more a matter of a loving
response to the husband's love.[13] Schlier provides no analysis of
ὑποτάσσω at either vv.22 or 24a, but does interpret the injunction to the
wife in terms of the analogies between the two relationships. The nature
of the analogies leads him to suggest that the wife's subordination is
exactly like that of the church. But he does not specify the nature of the
church's subordination.[14]

Other approaches appear more promising. Gnilka thinks that the
analogy between the two pairs suggests that the author desires to modify
the *Haustafel* taken from Col. 3.18 by injecting it with the teaching about
the mystery of the church (i.e., Eph. 5.31-32). Unfortunately, he does
not specify what he means by *"das Geheimnis Kirche"*.[15]But the idea that
the *Haustafel* is linked to the mystery of the church supports the thesis
that the injunction for subordination (vv.22-24) is very much related to
the "one flesh" unity of Christ and the church (v.31), which is called a
"mystery" at v.32.

The efforts of Barth and Cambier provide useful insights into the
nature of the wife's subordination. Barth's discussion focuses on the
nature of the action prescribed when ὑποτάσσω is invoked in the New
Testament. The basis of his argument is primarily lexical. He suggests
that two fundamental statements are made when the verb is used.[16] In

---

qualities or modifies the wife's subordination (i.e., obedience) to the husband ἐν παντί
(v.24b).
   [11] See *L'Épître*, pp. 210-211.
   [12] Following G. DELLING, *ThWNT*, VIII, pp. 40-42 and others, see SCHNACKEN-
BURG, *Der Brief*, p. 251, ns. 262-263.
   [13] See *Der Brief*, pp. 251-152.
   [14] See *Der Brief*, p. 254.
   [15] He writes, "Die Haustafel über die Ehe, die der Verf. aus Kol 3 holt, wird
benutzt zu einer nochmaligen Belehrung über das Geheimnis Kirche, das auch hier das
dem Verf. eigene Anliegen ausmacht." See *Epheserbrief*, p. 276.
   [16] The distinction between the subordination of believers and that of powers hostile
to God is commonplace, see BARTH, *Ephesians*, p. 710, n. 390. I would note that such a
distinction corresponds to the distinction between Christ's headship over the church and
his headship over hostile cosmological forces. Barth's analysis of subordination is greatly
indebted to D.S. BAILEY's, *The Mystery of Love and Marriage* (New York: Harper and
Row, 1952), pp. 129-136. The classic and still cogent statement concerning the distinction
between Christ's headship over the church and agents hostile to God is the work of

the active voice the verb expresses the ultimate power of God to bring forces hostile to God under divine control. Barth characterizes this kind of statement as the "order of right and might."[17] That is, the use of ὑποτάσσω and its cognates in the active voice signals God's power and might which overrides any individual freedom exercised by agents hostile to God.

Barth then notes that Paul applies ὑποτάσσω (as a verb, participle, as infinitive either in the middle or passive voices) when addressing the subordination of Christ, of church members, wives and so on.[18] Barth suggests that the use of the middle and passive voices "describes a voluntary attitude of giving in, cooperating, assuming responsibility, and carrying a burden."[19] He concludes that when ὑποτάσσω is applied in the passive but especially in the middle voice to the above mentioned groups, the action of subordination presupposes the activity of a morally free and responsible agent.[20] The implication of Barth's analysis is that the injunction for subordination is not a demand for a servile and spineless spouse. In light of Barth's analysis, the middle indicative ὑποτάσσεται at Eph. 5.24a suggests that the church willingly and freely subordinates herself to Christ. She is a morally free and responsible agent in her subordination.

In addition, Barth suggests that ὑποτάσσω expresses the idea of "order" in a fashion analogous to secular Greek military language (esp. in descriptions of battles), where the verb ὑποτάσσω and its cognates often describe various military strategies.[21] He then links this idea of "order" to the eschatological thrust of Ephesians. He summarizes his position by writing, "The eschatological expectation, the need to resist enemies [cf. Eph. 6.12] in the present evil day, and the missionary responsibility explain why a military term of all things received a central place in Paul's marriage counselling."[22]

Barth is correct to link the question of subordination to that of eschatology. Surely the church's mission to reveal God's plan of salva-

---

Cambier, "La seigneurie du Christ sur son Église et sur le monde," *Irénikon* 30 (1957):379-404.

[17] *Ephesians*, pp. 709-710. Barth lists the following texts: 1 Cor. 15.24-28; 54-55; Rom. 8.7, 20; Phil. 3.21; Col. 2.15; Eph. 1.21-22; 1 Pet. 3.22; Heb. 2.8; Lk. 10.17, 20.

[18] Ibid., p. 710. He lists the following texts: 1 Cor. 15.24-28, 54-55; Rom. 8.20, 38-39; Col. 2.15 and Eph. 1.19-21.

[19] *Ephesians*, p. 710.

[20] Ibid., p. 711. Delling (*TDNT*, VIII, p. 42) notes that when ὑποτάσσω occurs in the middle voice, except for Lk. 10.17 and 20, it always denotes voluntary subordination.

[21] BARTH cites H.G. LIDDELL and R. SCOTT, *A Greek-English Lexicon* (Oxford: Claredon Press, 1968), p. 1897, for examples of military contexts which contain ὑποτάσσω.

[22] See *Ephesians*, p. 711.

tion to the cosmological powers (cf. 3.10) is related to her subordination to Christ. No doubt the unity of the wife and husband in love does express the ethical goal of marriage and is one example of how believers fight not against blood and flesh but against "spiritual powers" (cf. 6.10-18). However, he does not pursue the suggestion that the wife's subordination expresses the same kind of dignity found in Christ's subordination to God (1 Cor. 15.28b). We shall return to this below.

According to Cambier, the injunction for subordination and the term κεφαλή signal the order of being initially established at Gen. 1-2, interpreted at 1 Cor. 11.3 and developed at Eph. 5.22-23 and especially 5.22-24.[23] Thus Cambier accounts for subordination in terms of the theological traditions underlying the use of the "head/subordination" tradition. These two marital roles are the consequences of being adopted children of God (Eph. 1.4-6), and are based on the believer's knowledge of the heavenly inheritance and the will of the Lord (5.17-21). Thus subordination is a free acceptance of divine order or of the ultimate plan of divine and salvific love.[24]

Cambier's analysis clearly points to what I thinks is the correct theological context for understanding subordination: subordination and headship have to do with God's intent for the New Creation. My own analysis confirms that of Cambier and supplements it by suggesting that the *Endzeit* model found in Jewish theological speculation about the eschatological Adam based on Gen. 1-2 appears to be the theological context from which to understand the "head/body" and "subordination" language. But like Barth, he does not push beyond the understanding that the church's subordination is the model for that of the wife.

In the previous chapter I argued that the points of contact between Eph. 1.19-23 and 1 Cor. 15.20-28 were numerous and significant enough to suggest that Eph. 1.19-23 develops Pauline theological reflections about Adam and Christ. Yet, we also noted that Eph. 1.19-23 seems to eliminate all explicit connections between Christ and Adam found at 1 Cor. 15.20-28. I then argued that several of the christological features at 1 Cor. 15.20-28 are present throughout Ephesians but are now transferred to the Church.[25] One critical element present in 1 Cor. 15.28b but absent at Eph. 1.19-23 is the subordination of Christ. I argued that this theological role was transferred to the church, along with other theological roles.[26]

---

[23] CAMBIER, "Le grand mystère concernant le Christ et son Eglise," pp. 58-59, 62, 66-67.

[24] Ibid., pp. 68-69.

[25] For example, Christ does battle with cosmological forces at 1 Cor. 15.24-25; in Ephesians it is the church who does battle (cf. 6.10-18).

[26] For example, at 1 Cor. 2.6-13 it is the spirit which reveals the wisdom of God (i.e., his plan of salvation). At Eph. 3.10 this role is given to the church.

I also argued that we could account for the restricted application of
ὑποτάσσω to the church at Eph. 5.24a on the basis that the author of
Ephesians wanted to link the subordination of the universal and cosmological church (e.g., 2.6) with that process of salvation described at 1
Cor. 15.20-28 — a process which unifies all things to God. In the case of
Ephesians, it is in the church and through Christ that such a process is
realized. That is, the church's subordination at Eph. 5.22-24 is modelled
on the role of Christ at 1 Cor. 15.20-28. It is precisely the subordination
of the New Adam — who is obedient to God to the point of death and
who is subordinate to God even in his resurrected status (1 Cor.
15.20-28) — which forms the theological model for the church's subordination.

The church's subordination therefore implies the following. First, it
participates in the process of salvation. The "body's" subordination to its
"head" expresses the initial realization of God's intent for redeemed
humanity. According to 1 Cor. 15.20-28 this intent ultimately unifies all
of creation to God. At 1 Cor. 15.20-28 this is done strictly through
Christ. At Eph. 5.24a and 3.10 the church is the instrument of reconciliation and unity. That is, the church's subordination represents the first
step in reconciling all things to God in Christ. That she is part of the New
Creation and therefore does represent this first step in reconciling all to
God is clear from the fact that her very creation (2.14-18), resurrected
status (2.6) and ongoing life in Christ (4.15-16) signals the eschatological
unity she enjoys with the the New Adam. Her subordination to the New
Adam suggests unity (i.e., they are "one flesh," Eph. 5.31-32) and
resurrected existence (cf. 2.6; 4.15-16) which empowers her in a number
of soteriological tasks.[27]

The eschatological and soteriological tradition behind subordination (i.e., 1 Cor. 15.28b) indicates that the church and, by analogy, the
wife both play a critical role in the saving process. The wife is not only
an adopted child of God, her married status establishes her as a critical
agent in the process of salvation. Her subordination to the husband
manifests on earth what is already accomplished in the heavenly places
in terms of the New Adam/Eve relationship (i.e., the "one flesh" unity
of Eph. 5.31-32). Her subordination reflects that of the New Eve.

In effect, both the wife and the husband are given christological
roles — they represent two unique expressions of what being in the
"image of Christ" can mean in marriage. The wife's subordination and
the husband's headship are rooted in two saving functions performed by

---

[27] The church "reveals" God's plan for salvation (3.10); she fights the cosmological
powers (6.10-20) and so on.

Christ. The husband's headship, at once a witness to God's creative gift to the wife and of Christ's agapic love, represents the role of Christ on the cross. Even if headship does not "save" the wife, it does represent how the husband enters into and gives witness to Christ's saving love.

The wife's subordination is modelled on the second of Christ's soteriological roles. Like Christ at 1 Cor. 15.28b, the wife's subordination is directed toward reconciling all things, beginning with Christian married relationships, to God. In Ephesians, this role is transferred to the church and by analogy to the wife. Both the subordination of the church and the wife affirms God's creative action, affirms eschatological unity and participates in the Christ/church "one flesh" unity of the New Creation.

Delling's summary of the meaning of ὑποτάσσω is most instructive at this point. He states that the presence of ὑποτάσσω in the middle voice throughout the New Testament but especially at Eph. 5.21 and 24 suggests that "the general rule demands readiness to renounce one's own will for the sake of others, i.e., ἀγάπη, and to give precedence to others."[28] For his part, the husband is exhorted to love[29] his wife as Christ loved the church and gave himself up for her (Eph. 5.25). Because the model for the husband's love is Christ's love for the church expressed on the cross, the demand is for the husband to, in the words of Delling, "renounce one's own will for the sake of others, i.e., ἀγάπη and to give precedence to others," especially the wife (in the context of Eph. 5.22-23).

The wife must be totally subordinate — that is, she must completely accept — the husband's Christ-like love and gift of self. The husband must love his wife completely, even to the point of his death. Both roles are christological, both roles demand total self-renunciation and both roles contribute to the soteriological process, manifesting the "one flesh" unity of Christ and the church, the New Adam and Eve of the New Creation.[30]

---

[28] DELLING, *TDNT*, VIII, p. 45.

[29] Note that ἀγάπη occurs at Eph. 5.25.

[30] Many have suggested that 5.21 may function as an introduction to the injunction for subordination and perhaps for the *Haustafel* as a whole. To the best of my knowledge no one has suggested how the idea of mutual subordination could be linked to an injunction which demands subordination only from the wife. Perhaps the mutual self-denial and total concern for the other spouse, through subordination (5.22) and through love (5.25), expresses the underlying dynamics of 5.21.

C. Exegetical Conclusions

1. Eph. 5.22-24 and 5.31

The central exegetical issue which prompted this study centers around the debate between J. Paul Sampley and A.T. Lincoln. The question was can the text of Eph. 5.31 be connected to the address to wives at Eph. 5.22-24? According to my reading of the text, the answer is yes. I have shown that the expansion of the address to wives was guided by a theological agenda which the author of Ephesians derived from Pauline and Jewish forms of theological reflection about the eschatological Adam.

The eschatological unity of the "head/body" language expresses what is already operative in the Christ/church relationship. It is Pauline language which has been pressed into the service of the author's theological agenda. The orientation of Eph. 5.22-24 is parenesis. The Pauline "head/body" language expresses the theological (1.19-23: "head"; 5.23c-24a: "body/church"; 2.6: "being raised by God"), and soteriological (5.23c: "he, savior of the body") frame of reference for that parenesis.

Because this Pauline "head/body" image is expressed in the form of parenesis, it is exhortation language, which encourages specific behavior. We should not let the theological frame of reference obscure the fact that the author is demanding concrete human behavior. Therefore, this action language represents the author's conception of the *manner in which* marriage can attain the eschatological unity of the New Adam and New Eve relationship. The *goal* of this marriage parenesis is the "one flesh" unity of Christ and the church. In order to make this crystal clear, the author cites the text of Gen. 2.24 at Eph. 5.31 and applies it to Christ and the church at v.32. The text of Eph. 5.31-32 expresses this goal in biblical imagery. It represents what the ethical behavior should achieve, namely, the "one flesh" unity of the New Adam and New Eve, that is, Eph. 5.22-24 expresses the *means* of entering into the New Creation. The text of Eph. 5.31-32 expresses the *goal* of the parenesis, the unity constitutive of the New Creation.

Lincoln's objections have been answered. It is by means of specifying the theological agenda guiding the use of Pauline language and Jewish forms of reflection about the eschatological Adam that we find a satisfactory answer to the debate.

2. The Use of the Ὑποτάσσω-*Torah Pattern*

Sampley's claim that the presence of ὑποτάσσω at Eph. 5.22, 24 and of Gen. 2.24 at Eph. 5.31 fits an early church literary pattern which connects the silence of women at the worships service or the subordination of wives to husbands to lessons from Torah is essentially correct.[31] However, there is need to make clear how the author of Ephesians modifies this literary convention by means of New Creation theology.

Although there is no *Urtext* behind the above mentioned literary pattern, we can isolate two of its essential characteristics. First, there is the basic exhortation to subordination and/or silence on the part of wives and/or women. Second, reference is made to an an example of the behavior intended, drawn from Torah.

For example, 1 Tim. 2.9-11 includes not one but several exhortations to women. They should dress modestly and be adorned in good works (vv.9-10), learn in silence and in all subordination. Verses 13-15 provide two arguments from Torah which offer justification for the injunction. First, the argument about the "order of being" is given: Adam was formed first, then Eve (v.14). Second, Eve was deceived, not Adam (v.15). Here, the injunction for subordination is connected with a negative rationale. Women cannot do "x" because of "y" and "z" in Torah. In particular, the order of creation and Eve's role in the first sin are the decisive factors in this rationale.[32]

The second clear example of this pattern is 1 Pet. 3.1-6. Here we have the traditional exhortation for subordination (v.1) followed by several types of justification. First, wives ought to be subordinate because such behavior could convert others (1b-2). There follows a second type of rationale, one which describes an accompanying internal disposition "proper" to subordination (vv.3-4). Then, a lesson from Torah (vv.5-6). The "holy women" (v.5) and esp. Sarah (v.6) hoped in God and were subordinate to their husbands. In this instance it is not Eve but another figure from Genesis who illustrates the behavior expected of the Christian wife.

In both instances, the examples are drawn from the *past*, from the Torah. This concern with sacred history is not surprising since the Scriptures are often cited in arguments to support this or that theological contention throughout the Pauline Corpus. In addition there was much latitude for creative assimilation of these past traditions. In the example from 1 Tim. 2, the rationale for subordination appeals to a time prior to

---

[31] *One Flesh*, pp. 96-102, 114-177.

[32] It is not all that clear to me how 2 Cor. 11.1-4 fits this pattern, as Sampley would have us think, see *One Flesh*, p. 98. The text neither argues for the subordination of the wife nor gives a justification for the community's "subordination" to Paul or anyone else. Sampley stretches the point when he writes "The Christians are portrayed as the wife from whom purity is expected, but is afraid that this wife [i.e., the Corinthian community] is about to be led astray into a misplaced submission to 'another' gospel." Ibid.

the fall (i.e., Adam existed first, then Eve) and to a time during the fall (the deception of Eve). At 1 Pet. 3.5-6 the author appeals to Sarah's holiness and hope in God. The text of 1 Peter thus represents a positive reference to Torah while 1 Timothy contains both positive and negative forms of rationale.

At Eph. 5.22, 24 and 31 we see a similar pattern, but with significant differences. First, even though the author perpetuates the injunction for subordination, he modifies such an injunction by not applying the verb ὑποτάσσω *directly* to the wife thus making the church's subordination paradigmatic for that of the wife. Second, the author has not abandoned the "reference to Torah" since at Eph. 5.32 he makes clear that the text of Gen. 2.24 refers to the church.

It is striking that the example for the wife's subordination still contains a reference to Torah but not with reference to *past* sacred history. The text of Eph. 5.22-23 significantly modifies the pattern because the wife's example is now a living and dynamic organism, the church. In this instance reference is not made to women of the *past* or to *Urzeit* Eve but to the *Endzeit* New Eve of the New Creation. The collective subordination of the New Eve to the New Adam functions much like the "enacted parables" in the prophetic corpus. That is, it is the ongoing and historical example of the church's subordination to Christ from which the wife must derive an understanding of her subordination. The mutual subordination of men to men, women to women, men to women and women to men as well as those activities listed at 5.18-21 form the *Endzeit* matrix for subordination. The example is no longer taken from sacred stories of the *past*; it is to be taken from the *contemporary* experience of the New Eve, who reverses the sacred story about the first Eve.

3. Adam in Paul and Ephesians

Many have noted the importance of explicit and implicit references to Genesis or Adam and Eve throughout the undisputed letters of Paul.[33] Whenever Paul makes explicit reference to Adam (1 Cor. 15.21-22, 45-49; Rom. 5.14) or Eve (2 Cor. 11.3), he does so negatively. His use of Gen. 2.24 functions otherwise. At 1 Cor. 6.16 he cites this text as an illustration of the unity between Christ and the believer which in turn is an argument against the union of a believer with a prostitute. Intercourse with a prostitute would in effect join Christ to that prostitute (cf. vv.14-15). Although Gen. 2.24 functions in terms of a polemic against πορνεία, it is still a positive reference.

The author of Ephesians extends this positive understanding of Gen. 2.24 at Eph. 5.31. In good Pauline fashion, he refrains from explicitly naming Christ as "'Αδάμ" and the church as "Εὔα." Yet, he also modifies the Pauline tradition in that the citation and explicit application of Gen. 2.24 to the Christ/church relationship (vv.31-32) clearly expresses his intent to link Christ and the church with the New Adam and New Eve of the New Creation. This kind of theological reflection stands closer to the *Urzeit/Endzeit* pattern so often encountered in Jewish literature prior to and after the advent of Christianity, as we have already seen.

That is, the biblical Adam and Eve are given "good press" in Ephesians. Adam is no longer an anti-type of Christ (e.g., 1 Cor. 15.21-22) and Eve is no longer the "one who is deceived" (e.g., 2 Cor. 11.3). Rather, they represent the re-creation of humanity; they are paradigms for *Endzeit* or eschatological humanity. This represents a significant shift in Pauline theological reflection. Perhaps the author refrains from explicitly connecting Christ with Adam and the church with Eve because of the respect he obviously shows for the letters of Paul, which by this date appear to be a theological-linguistic resource for subsequent Christian theologians in the "Pauline trajectory."[34] Yet clearly the author felt free to modify and extend Pauline thought, apparently without betraying any of the genuine insights from the master.

4. Does Eph. 5.22-24 Stand With or Against Its Culture

This study can be best characterized as literary-theological. I have attempted to reconstruct the theological agenda which may have guided the expansion of a first century Christian text. Whether or not Eph. 5.22-24 stands with or against its culture is formally another question. Even so, I offer the following by way of a preliminary answer.

Based on my interpretation of Eph. 5.22-24, my proposition is that the address to wives does challenge certain aspects of what most scholars would correctly see as an androcentric and patriarchal culture. I say "certain aspects" because clearly the text does not reject the androcentric conceptual frame of reference. For example, the injunction for the wife's subordination is typically androcentric: wives are subordinate to husbands. The argument that the church's subordination is derived from Christ's subordination also fits an androcentric thought structure: the female's action (symbolized by the church) is patterned after a male's

---

[33] E.g., STANLEY, "Paul's Interest in the Early Chapters of Genesis," pp. 241-252.

[34] Respect for Pauline tradition can be seen in texts where the days of the "holy apostles" are long gone, see Eph. 4.11; 5.3. Paul normally describes his preaching to the Gentiles without reference to it being done by him through a church. Such is not the picture presented at 3.1-13; it is now the job of the church which is founded on, among other things, the apostles and prophets (2.10).

action (i.e., Christ's subordination to God). In addition, the rationale for subordination is androcentrically conceived. As we saw in the second chapter, the logical flow of the address as well as its chiastic structure indicate that the whole text is centered around 5.23c: "he, savior of the body," a soteriological statement about a male.

In other words, it is important to understand that the presuppositions of the writer and readers of this text clearly stand within an androcentric frame of reference. To claim anything else would be to misunderstand the text and its cultural context. Therefore, the issue is not whether or not the author flatly rejects an androcentric mindset. It is a question of how he challenges some of its elements. How, then, does this text challenge "certain aspects" of androcentric culture?

My proposal is that although the author thinks within an androcentric frame of reference, he nonetheless radically changes its orientation by changing the meaning of the subordination and headship language. Thus while he maintains an androcentric conceptual structure, he rejects its potential for domination, especially within husband and wife relationships.

The clearest example of this kind of challenge to the androcentric mindset is at Eph. 5.25, where the husband is exhorted to love the wife as Christ loved the church and gave himself up for her. We have already noted how Fiorenza understands this injunction. She notes that husbands are exhorted to love their wives three times (5.25, 28, 33). The net result is that 5.25 represents a theological modification of the patriarchal-societal code. "Patriarchal domination is thus radically questioned with reference to the paradigmatic love relationship of Christ to the church."[35] To Fiorenza's analysis I would add that whatever prior understanding a first century Mediterranean Christian husband might have had about his role in the family, clearly the author links such a role to Christ's agapic, other-centered love which by definition must exclude the element of domination within human relationships. The husband cannot dominate the wife under these circumstances. If he did, he would not be expressing Christ's agapic love.

The patriarchal structure remains intact (i.e., the wife is subordinate to the husband), but the dynamics within that structure are radically refocused on the wife's well-being. This agapic love is fundamental to the role and internal disposition of the husband. For our purposes, this part of the *Haustafel* functions as an heuristic device which offers preliminary confirmation that indeed the author of Ephesians does critique the aspect of domination of husband over wife.

The absence of the verb at vv.22 and 24b and the emphasis on the

---

[35] "In Memory of Her," pp. 269-270.

church's subordination to Christ represent the first clues that the reader should not take things at face value. According to my interpretation of the church's subordination to Christ, her action is that of a free, willing and responsible agent in the process of salvation which brings about the New Creation. She accepts the husband's Christ-like love as God's gift to her which also draws her into the salvation process. The wife's role in the New Creation also reverses the role of the first Eve by doing battle with the forces of darkness (Eph. 6.10-20), forces which until the eschatological age had the power to deceive her. Unlike any other women in the Scriptures, she and the New Adam mediate to the cosmos the plan of reconciliation and of uniting all things in Christ. Like Christ's subordination to God, the New Eve's subordination is an essential step in the process of salvation.

According to Eph. 5.22-25, subordination is not simply obedience to a despot, nor is it something the wife does by coercion, at the behest of cultural traditions in step with social stereotypes. Her subordination or willingness to accept the husband's agapic love "in everything" (5.24) indicates that she accepts her husband's love as a gift from God. Her "subordination" to the husband also contributes to the eschatological unity already experienced in the Christ/church relationship.

By redefining subordination and headship in terms of New Creation theology, the author of Ephesians has dislodged androcentric marriage from its powerbase of domination and relocated it in the sphere of discipleship which participates in and makes a contribution to the New Creation. Marriage is no longer a question of the "stronger" versus the "weaker"; it is no longer a question of the "ruler" over the "ruled." Because marriage is now linked to the process of reconciliation and uniting, the process of salvation which brings about New Creation and which must be manifest in Christian marriage.

If the message of Ephesians is founded on the goal of uniting all things, in Christ (1.10), and if this goal is already realized in the Christ/church relationship (1.22-23; 2.6; 4.15-16; 5.31-32), then the unity and love of the wife/husband relationship stands as an important realization of that goal and is at once a rejection of any dehumanizing elements present in androcentric or patriarchal culture. The wife/husband relationship also represents a re-creation of human dignity because Christian marriage now stands against the impulse to dominate and control. Now it must manifest how agapic love reconstitutes, recreates, reconciles and unifies. As such it represents a human dynamic which, transformed by the spirit of Christ, gives witness to the process in which all things are united in Christ.

D. **Hermeneutical Reflections**

We live in an age of human rights and civil liberties. People have and are giving their lives for these rights and liberties. How can a text written several centuries ago, from an androcentric worldview, which calls for the "subordination" of wives speak to our cultural climate?

The text is deceptively simple. It contains all of the trappings of an androcentric worldview and could easily be misunderstood as a justification of patriarchal domination. It is very much a "sheep in wolf's clothing." It must therefore be read in light of its theological message about the power of living for others rather than as a justification for male domination, itself an absolute contradiction to the very nature of agapic love. It would be a serious mistake to think that contemporary men and women have surpassed their ancestors and put to rest once and for all domination and oppression. On the contrary, there is still much work to be done. It is precisely because this text expects selflessness, sacrificial and agapic love from the Christian husband and exhorts the Christian wife to freely choose to accept this Christ-like love from *within an androcentric worldview* that its message is not only relevant but necessary for this day and age. By addressing the dilemma of first century androcentric domination the text also speaks to twentieth century domination.

The text of Eph. 5.22-24 has much to teach women and men about Christian marriage. What it teaches is neither idyllic nor idealistic because it speaks directly to the androcentric mindset, reinterpreting it and freeing it from its dehumanizing elements. The text does not first create a theoretical world and then explain, in principle, how wives and husbands ought to act. Rather, the text directly addresses and challenges androcentric domination by redefining androcentric power language in terms of agapic love. The text challenges androcentric domination by stating that other-centered love and human dignity are possible for both spouses, *even* in an androcentric setting. The tension between human dignity and dehumanizing androcentricism found at Eph. 5.22-33 could be described as a collision of two worldviews, where the brilliance of agapic love pushes the darkness of domination and oppression into retreat.

The theological context of the address to wives is not idealistic because it understands and addresses the very core of human existence, the domicile of dispair, hope, love, hate, and the impulse to dominate and control. The text understands us, perhaps better than we have understood it. The "Achilles heel" of human existence, the power of sin in our lives, prevents us from giving ourselves to God, our brothers and sisters in Christ, and to our spouses. Sin does not only prevent us giving ourselves in personal relationships, it also controls how we act in them.

When we relate to others in the presence of fear, the absence of trust and the experience of alienation, the core of our human experience easily lends itself to domination and control.

The potential for being hurt, abused, disrespected, betrayed as well as the potential for being accepted, affirmed, loved, healed and set free is greatest within interdependent relationships where the deepest and most intimate human vulnerabilities and needs surface. It is precisely here where wife and husband might know the temptation to dominate, betray, destroy, or, to create, love and give the self to the other. The text addresses this core of human experience with a message of hope: the giving and receiving of agapic love has the power not just to heal, but to take the husband and wife from brokenness to wholeness; it holds out the promise to re-create both spouses into the image of the New Adam and New Eve. The re-creating occurs in the depths of human experience, where the power to live the challenge of giving and receiving agapic love must find its home.

This theological agenda is not a matter of idealism. Rather, it takes very seriously the concrete impact which domination and oppression have on the hidden and interior but nevertheless real life of the individual. It addresses this very real core of human experience. The exhortation to freely give and receive agapic love involves human relationships and therefore social reality. The challenge to talk, walk, eat, and in general, interact with other humans *in love* radically calls into question a concrete social reality, the domination of wives by their husbands. Yet it is also a call to the imagination, where spouses are to shake off "the dust of the world" from their eyes and form or, perhaps better, reconstruct a social reality based on loving each other. The model of Christ and the church — made concrete in the experience of Christians living in a community grounded in love — functions as the fundamental starting point, prompting the imagination to "see" what is possible.

It is the life in the Spirit which empowers those wounded and sick to see that the New Adam and Eve present a message of hope and therefore an alternative to a lifestyle based on an experience which either seeks to dominate or to avoid domination. The Christ/church relationship, built and sustained on agapic self-giving, demythologizes and remythologizes power so that it now enables and sets free.

In more traditional Christian language, this remythologizing process is called evangelization and conversion, where the believer is called to leave the power trappings of "the world" and enter into an experience in which God heals, restores, re-creates, sets free and empowers both spouses to love as Christ loved. Texts from Sacred Scripture which speak to this agenda are sacred precisely because they reveal God's saving action in the experience and thought of earlier generations who were empowered by God to live the gospel.

In other words, this text can function as a moment of evangelism and conversion within the life of the church. As a moment of evangelism, its proclamation or announcement is of freedom which at once is a rejection of domination. As a moment of conversion it can free the wife and husband from the bondage which the "ruler/ruled" and "stronger/weaker" dynamics create in individuals. It challenges both spouses to become freed from the power of sin (which stops them from fully giving themselves to each other), to become the servant of the other, to have as the highest priority the well-being of the other. It is a challenge to test whether or not giving and receiving Christ's agapic love frees from selfishness, selfcenteredness and the bondage of inner wounds and whether or not spouses can exercise a freedom which re-creates, empowers and enables them to make a total gift of self to the other, just as Christ and the church do to each other. It is a challenge to seek and discover the New Creation in Christ through marriage.

The lifestyle of living for the other, where mutual openness, trust, love and self-denial exist, is what challenges the core of human experience. These elements not only free the individual from the impulse of revenge or domination, they also can empower the individual to forgive and reconcile. These elements represent part of the human reality behind what being filled with the spirit means, something quite necessary for married life, as the text of 5.18-21 makes clear.

This lifestyle of being filled with the spirit is the new locus of power. It is a power which frees the wife and husband from the dehumanizing power struggle of the "ruler/ruled" and "stronger/weaker" patriarchal and androcentric social dynamics. Spouses need no longer struggle to dominate or to avoid being dominated. Through subordination and headship and living for the well-being of the other both spouses enter into a realm of freedom which transfers them from the world of darkness into the realm of light, where they become "children of the light" (5.8). Agapic love empowers the husband to live for the wife's well-being at the cost of personal desire, comfort and personal preference. The wife's subordination receives the husband's empowered act of selfless love with joy, as a gift from God. When spouses give and receive each other as free gifts of Christ's love, the impulse to dominate is replaced with a new found capacity to forgive and reconcile, which is itself part of the process of freely giving one's self to the other. This lifestyle of discipleship is a call to leave the power of "the world" behind; it is a call to be filled with the spirit and its consequent empowerment which frees the depths of human existence from sin, domination and darkness. This lifestyle ultimately produces the eschatological unity already manifest in the New Adam and New Eve relationship, and is needed today.

Bibliography

ALAND, K., NESTLE, E. *Novum Testamentum Graece*[26]. Stuttgart: Deutsche Bibelgesellschaft, 1979.

ABBOTT, T.K. *A Critical and Exegetical Commentary on the Epistles to the Ephesians and to the Colossians*. ICC. Edinburgh: T. & T. Clark, [1897] 1979.

ANDRIESSEN, P. "La nouvelle Ève, corps du nouvel Adam." In *Aux Origines de l'Église*. ed. J. Giblet et. al. Recherches Bibliques VII Louvain: Desclée de Brouwer, 1965.

BAILEY, D.S. *The Mystery of Love and Marriage*. New York: Harper and Row, 1952.

BALCH, D.J. *Let Wives be Submissive: The Domestic Code in 1 Peter*. SBLMS 26 Chico, CA.: Scholars Press, 1981.

BARRETT, C.K. *A Commentary on the Epistle to the Romans*. HNTC. New York: Harper and Row, 1957.

idem. *A Commentary on the First Epistle to the Corinthians*. HNTC. New York: Harper and Row, 1968.

BARTH, M. *Ephesians*. AB 34-34A. Garden City, New York: Doubleday & Company, Inc., 1974.

BEARE, F.W. "Epistle to the Ephesians." *Interpreters Bible*. ed. G.A. Buttrick. Nashville: Abingdon Press, 1953.

BEDALE, S. "The meaning of κεφαλή in the Pauline Epistles." *JTS* 5 (1954): 911-915.

BENOIT, P. "Corps, tête et plérôme dans les Épître de la captivité." *RB* 63 (1956):5-44.

BEST, E. *One Body in Christ; a Study of the Relationship of the to Christ in the Epistles of the Apostle Paul*. London: S.P.C.K., 1955.

BORNKAMM, G. S.v. "μυστήριον" *Theological Dictionary of the New Testament*, IV, p. 823.

BRANDENBURGER, E. *Adam und Christus*. WMANT 7. Neukirchen: Neukirchener Verlag, 1962.

BROOTEN, B.J. *Women Leaders in the Ancient Synagogues: Inscriptional Evidence and Background Issues*. Brown Judaic Series 36. Chico, C.A.: Scholars Press, 1982.

BROWN, RAYMOND E. *The Semitic Background of the Term "Mystery" in the New Testament*. Facet Books, Biblical Series 21 Philadelphia: Fortress Press, 1968.

BURNEY, C.F. "Christ as the 'APXH of Creation (Prov. VIII 22, Col. I 15-18, Rev. III 14)," *JTS* 27 (1926):160-177.

CAMBIER, J. "Le grand mystère concernant le Christ et son Église." *Bib* 47 (1966):43-90.

idem. "La seigneurie du Christ sur son Église et sur le monde" *Irénikon* 30 (1957):379-404.

CARAGOUNIS, CHRYS, C. *The Ephesian Mysterion: Meaning and Content.* Lund: CWK Gleerup, 1977.

CHARLESWORTH, J.H. *The Pseudepigrapha and Modern Research.* SBLSBS 7. Missoula, Montana: Scholars Press, 1976.

idem. The Old Testament Pseudepigrapha. 2 vols. Garden City, New York: Doubleday, 1984-1985.

COLPE, C. "Zur Leib-Christi-Verstellung im Epheserbrief." in *Judentum, Christentum, Kirche.* ed. W. Eltester. BZNW 26. Berlin: Töpelmann, 1960.

idem. Die religionsgeschichtliche Schule. Göttingen: Vandenhoeck und Ruprecht, 1961.

CONZELMANN, H. *1 Corinthians.* Trans. J.W. Leitch. Philadelphia: Fortress Press, 1975.

COUTTS, J. "The Relationship between Ephesians and Colossians." *NTS* 4 (1958):201-207.

CROUCH, J. *The Origin and Intention of the Colossian Haustafel.* FRLANT 109. Göttingen: Vandenhoeck and Ruprecht, 1971.

DAHL, N.A. "Christ, Creation and the Church." *The Background of the New Testament and its Eschatology.* W.D. Davies and D. Daube eds. Cambridge: The University Press, 1956.

idem. "Cosmic Dimensions and Religious Knowledge (Eph. 3:18)." eds. E.E. Ellis and E. Grasser. *Jesus und Paulus.* Göttingen: Vandenhoeck und Ruprecht, 1975.

DANA, H.E. and J.R. MANTEY, *A Manual of the Greek New Testament.* New York: The McMillan Co., 1944.

DAUTZENBURG, G. et. al. *Die Frau im Urchristentum.* QD 95. Freiburg/Basel/Wein: Herder, 1983.

DAVIES, W.D. *Paul and Rabbinic Judaism: Some Rabbinic Elements in Pauline Theology.* Philadelphia: Fortress Press, (1948) 1981.

DELLING, G. S.v. "ὑποτάσσω" *Theological Dictionary of the New Testament*, VIII, pp. 39-45.

DIBELIUS, M. *An die Kolosser, Epheser an Philemon.* 3 Auflage. Tübingen: J.C.B. Mohr (John Siebeck), [1936] 1953.

DUBARLE, A.M. "L'origine dans l'Ancien Testament de la notion paulinienne de l'Église Corps du Christ." *Studiorum Paulinorum Congressus Internationalis Catholicus.* AnBib 17 Rome: Pontifical Biblical Institute Press, 1962.

FIORENZA, SCHÜSSLER, E. *In Memory of Her: A Feminist Theological Reconstruction of Christian Origins.* New York: Crossroad, 1983.

FOERSTER, W. S.v. "σωτήρ" *Theological Dictionary of the New Testament*, VII, pp. 1003-1012, 1013-1022, 1023-1024.

FOHRER, G. S.v. "σωτήρ" *Theological Dictionary of the New Testament*, VII, pp. 1012-1013, 1022-1023.

GNILKA, J. *Der Epheserbrief.* HTKNT 10.2 Freiburg: Herder, 1971.

GUNKEL, H. *Schöpfung und Chaos in Urzeit*. Göttingen: Vandenhoeck und Ruprecht, 1895.

GRUDEM, W. "Appendix 1: Does *kephalē* ('head') Mean 'Source' or 'Authority Over' in Greek Literature? A Survey of 2,336 Examples." G. Knight III ed. *The Role Relationship between Men and Women*. Revised Edition. Moody Press, 1985, pp. 43-68.

HANSON, S. *The Unity of the Church in the New Testament, Colossians and Ephesians*. ASNU 14. Uppsala: Almquist, 1946.

HENDRIKSEN, W. *Exposition of Ephesians*. NTC 2. Grand Rapids, Mich.: Baker Book House, 1967.

HENGEL, M. *Judaism and Hellenism*. 2 vols. Philadelphia: Fortress Press, 1974.

HORSLEY, R.A. "Pneumatikos vs. Psychikos: Distinctions of Spiritual Status among the Corinthians." *HTR* 69 (1967):269-288.

HOULDEN, J.L. *Paul's Letters from Prison: Philippians, Colossians, Philemon, and Ephesians*. Westminster Pelican Commentaries. Philadelphia: Westminster, (1970) 1977.

HOWARD, G. "The Head/Body Metaphors of Ephesians." *NTS* 20 (1974):350-356.

JERVELL, J. *Imago Dei. Gen. 1,26f. im Spätjudentum, in der Gnosis und in den paulinischen Briefen*. FRLANT 76. Göttingen: Vandenhoeck & Ruprecht, 1960.

KANJUPARAMBIL, P. "Imperative Participles in Rom 12:9-21." *JBL* 102 (1983):285-288.

KÄSEMANN, E. "Ephesians and Acts." *Studies in Luke-Acts*. L.E. Keck and J.L. Martyn eds. Nashville: Abingdon Press, 1966.

idem. Leib und Leib Christi. Tübingen: J.B.C. Mohr (Paul Siebeck) 1933.

idem. "Das Interpretationsproblem des Epheserbriefes." *TLZ* 86 (1961):1-8.

KECK, L.E. et. al. eds. *Studies in Luke-Acts*. Nashiville: Abingdom Press, 1966.

KNOX, W.L. *St Paul and the Church of the Gentiles*. Cambridge: Cambridge University Press, 1939.

KUHN, K.G. "Der Epheserbrief im Lichte der Qumrantexte." *NTS* 7 (1961):334-346.

LEIPOLDT, J. *Die Frau in der antiken Welt und im Urchristentum*. Gütersloh, 1962.

LIDDELL, H.G. and SCOTT, R. et. al. *A Greek-English Lexicon*. Oxford: Clarendon Press, 1968.

LINCOLN, A.T. "The use of the OT in Ephesians [Gen. 2.24; Ex. 20.12; Is. 57.19 & Ps. 68.18]." *JSNT 14* (1982):16-57.

LINDARS, B. *New Testament Apologetics*. London: SCM Press, 1961.

LOHSE, E. *Colossians and Philemon*. Philadelphia: Fortress Press, 1971.

LUND, N.W. *Chiasmus in the New Testament: A Study of Formgeschichte*. Chapel Hill: The University of North Carolina Press, 1942.

MALINA, B. Review of *The First Urban Christians: The Social World of the Apostle Paul*, by W.A. Meeks. *JBL* 104 (1985):346-347.

MARTIN, R.P. "An epistle in search of a life-setting." *ExpTim* 79 (1968):296-302.

MASSON, C. *L'Épître de Saint Paul aux Éphésiens*. Paris/Neuchatel: Delachaux & Niestlé S.A., 1953.

MEEKS, W.A. *The First Urban Christians: The Social World of the Apostle Paul.* New Haven/London: Yale University Press, 1983.

MITTON, C.L. *The Epistle to the Ephesians: Its Authorship, Origin and Purpose.* Oxford: The Clarendon Press, 1951.

idem. Ephesians. NCB. Grand Rapids, Mich.: Eerdmans, 1981.

MUNRO, W. "Col. iii.18-iv.1 and Eph. v.21-vi.9: Evidences of Late Literary Stratum?" *NTS* 18 (1972):434-447.

MURAOKA, T. "The Use of ΩΣ in the Greek Bible." *NovT* 7 (1964):51-72.

MUSSNER, F. *Christus, Das All und Die Kirche: Studien zum Theologie des Epheserbriefes.* Trier Theologische Studien 5. Trier: Paulinus Verlag, 1955.

ORR, W.F. WALKER, J.A. *1 Corinthians,* AB 32 (Garden City, N.J.: Doubleday and Company, Inc., 1976.

PERCY, E. *Der Leib Christi in den paulinischen Homologomena und Antilogomena.* Lund: Universitets Arsschrift, 1942.

PERRIN, N. "The Use of *(Para)didonai* in Connection with the Passion of Jesus in the New Testament." *idem, A Modern Pilgrimage in New Testament Christology.* Philadelphia: Fortress Press, 1974.

PLUMMER, A. and ROBERTSON, A. *A Critical and Exegetical Commentary on the First Epistle of St. Paul to the Corinthians².* ICC. Edinburgh: T. & T. Clark, 1914.

RAMAROSON, L. "'L'Église, corps du Christ' dans les écrits pauliniens: simples esquisses, *ScEs* 30 (1978):129-141.

RENGSTORF, K.H. "Die neutestamentlichen Mahnungen an die Frau, sich dem Manne unterzuordnen." *Verbum Dei manet in aeternum. Festschrift für O. Schmitz.* Witten: Luther Verlag, 1953, pp. 131-145.

ROBERTSON, A. PLUMMER, A. *A Critical and Exegetical (Commentary on the First Epistle of St. Paul to the Corinthians².* ICC. Edinburgh: T. & T. Clark, 1914.

ROBINSON, A.T. *A Grammar of the Greek New Testament in Light of Historical Research.* Nashiville: Broodmans Press, 1934.

ROBINSON, J.A. *St. Paul's Epistle to the Ephesians².* London: J. Clarke & Co. Ltd., 1922.

ROBINSON, J.M. "Die Hodajot-Formel in Gebet und Hymnus des Früchristentums." *Apophoreta; Festschrift für Ernst Haenchen.* Berlin: Alfred Töpelmann, 1964.

ROON, VAN, A. *The Authenticity of Ephesians.* Trans. S. Proscod-Jokel. Leiden: E.J. Brill, 1974.

ROSS, J.T. *The Conception of ΣΩTHPIA in the New Testament.* Ph.D. dissertation, University of Chicago, 1947.

SAMPLEY, J. Paul. *And the Two Shall Become one Flesh.* SNTSMS 16 Cambridge: University Press, 1971.

SCHLIER, H. *Der Brief an die Epheser.* Düsseldorf: Patmos-Verlag, 1957.

idem. and WARNACH, V. *Die Kirche im Epheserbrief.* Münster: Aschendorff, 1949.

SCHLIER, H. *Christus und die Kirche in Epheserbrief.* Tübingen: J.B.C. Mohr (Paul Siebeck), 1933.

SCHNACKENBURG, R. *Der Brief an die Epheser.* EKKNT 10. Zürich/Einsiedeln/Köln: Benzinger, 1982.

SCHWEIZER, E. "Die Kirche als Leib Christi in den paulinischen Antilegomena."
    TLZ 86 (1961): 241-256.
idem. The Letter to the Colossians. Trans. A. Chester. Minneapolis, MN.:
    Augsburg Publishing House, 1982.
SCHWEITZER, A. *The Mysticism of Paul the Apostle.* New York: Holt, 1931.
SCOTT, E.F., *The Epistle to the Colossians, to Philemon and to the Ephesians.*
    MNTC. London: Hodder and Stoughton, 1930.
SCROGGS, R. *The Last Adam.* Philadelphia: Fortress Press, 1966.
idem. "Paul and the Eschatological Wowan" *JAAR* XL (1972):283-303.
idem. S.v. "Women in the N.T." *IDBSup*, pp. 966-968.
SMITH, D.C. *Jewish and Greek Traditions in Ephesians 2:11-22.* Ph.D. disserta-
    tion, Yale University, 1970.
idem. "The Two Made One: Some Observations on Eph. 2.14-18." *OJRS* 1
    (1973):34-54.
STAERK, W. *Der Erlösererwartung in den Östichen Regligionen. Untersuchungen
    zu den Ausdrucksformen der Biblischen Soteriologie (Soter II).* Stuttgart
    und Berlin, 1938.
STANLEY, D.M. "Paul's Interest in the Early Chapters of Genesis." *Studiorum
    Paulinorum Congressus Internationalis Catholicus.* AnBib 17-18
    (1963):241-252.
STENDAHL, K. *The Bible and the Role of Women. A Case Study in Hermeneutics.*
    Trans. E.T. Sander. Facet Books, Biblical Series 15. Philadelphia: Fortress
    Press, 1966.
STUHLMACHER, P. *Historical Criticism and Theological Interpretation of Scrip-
    ture.* Trans. R.A. Harrisville. Philadelphia: Fortress Press, 1977.
TURNER, N. *A Grammar of New Testament Greek.* Volume III. Edinburgh: T. &
    T. Clark, 1963.
USAMI, KŌSHI. *Somatic Comprehension of Unity: The Church in Ephesus.*
    AnBib 101. Rome: Pontifical Biblical Institute Press, 1983.
WALKER, W.O. Jr. "The 'Theology of Women's Place' and the 'Paulinist'
    Tradition." *Semeia* 28 (1983):101-112.
WEDDERBURN, A.J.M. "Adam in Paul's Letter to the Romans." *Studia Biblica*
    III (1978):413-430.
WILD, R. "The Warrior and the Prisoner: Some Reflections on Ephesians
    6:10-20." *CBQ 46* (1984):284-298.
idem. "'Be imitators of God': Discipleship in the Letter to the Ephesians."
    Chapter 6 in *Discipleship in the New Testament.* ed. F.F. Segovia.
    Philadelphia: Fortress Press, 1985.

General Index

Hebrew Words

Greek Words

134

GENERAL INDEX

5.17: 51, 87
9.10: 47
10.15: 47
11.1-4: 111
11.2-3: 94
11.3: 112-3

Gal.
2.20: 52, 55
3.28: 9

Eph.
1.3: 53, 91
1.4: 60
1.4-6: 107
1.7: 53
1.9: 78
1.10: 87, 91-2, 95-6, 115
1.13: 53
1.15: 47
1.16: 47
1.17: 83, 89
1.19: 47, 101
1.19-20: 77, 89-91
1.19-21: 106
1.19-23: 69, 77-9, 80-6, 88, 91, 101, 107, 110
1.20: 47, 78-9, 81-2, 91
1.20-22: 88
1.21: 47, 72, 80
1.21-22: 80-1, 106
1.22: 46, 67, 70-2, 75, 78-9, 81-4, 90-1, 95
1.22-23: 46-7, 50-2, 65, 72, 77-8, 84, 89, 115
1.23: 46, 70, 78, 84
2: 47
2.5: 53, 62
2.5-6: 88, 90
2.6: 81, 90-1, 95, 102, 108, 110, 115
2.7: 53
2.8: 53
2.10: 51, 61, 84, 87, 101, 113
2.11-12: 55
2.11-13: 55
2.11-14: 47
2.11-22: 6, 47, 54, 60
2.13: 53
2.13-18: 62
2.14: 55, 62-3
2.14-15: 56, 61-2, 101
2.14-16: 55, 83-5, 87, 101
2.14-18: 6, 21, 45, 55-6, 63-4, 66, 85, 108, 123

2.15: 47, 51, 55-6, 60-4, 87, 89, 90, 92, 95-6
2.15-16: 51, 55, 84, 87
2.16: 47, 55
2.19-22: 47, 55
2.21: 47
2.22: 47
3.1-13: 113
3.2: 83
3.7-8: 83
3.10: 89-91, 95, 107-8
3.18: 120
4.1-3: 12
4.1-16: 71
4.2-3: 89
4-6: 32
4.5: 32
4.7: 71
4.7-8: 83
4.11: 71, 83, 113
4.13: 47, 51, 71, 90
4.14: 47
4.15: 67, 71-2, 90
4.15-16: 47, 50, 65, 70-5, 77, 89-92, 95, 108, 115
4.16: 47, 67, 71, 84
4.23-24: 51
5: 34
5.1: 34, 36
5.2: 52, 54-5
5.3: 113
5.3-4: 89
5.8: 32, 34, 36, 118
5.10: 32
5.15-21: 89
5.17: 13-5, 32, 98
5.17-21: 14, 49, 90, 97-8, 104, 107
5.17.22: 104
5.18: 28-9, 36, 49, 98
5.18-21: 112, 118
5.18-22: 98
5.19: 32
5.21: 2, 11, 13, 21, 25-9, 32, 36-7, 48-9, 77, 98, 101, 104, 109
5.21-22: 103
5.22: 2, 5, 7, 10-5, 21, 23, 25-44, 48, 49-50, 77, 92, 97-9, 101-5, 109-110, 112, 114
5.22-23: 49, 77-8, 107-8, 112
5.22-24: 2, 5-10, 12-13, 15-9, 21, 23-6, 29-30, 32, 34, 40, 41, 44-50, 52, 64, 66-7, 69, 75, 77, 79, 84, 95-7, 103, 105, 107-8, 110, 113, 116
5.22-25: 115
5.22-33: 6, 8, 16, 23-4, 35, 46, 48, 55, 84, 116

5.22-6.9: 6, 27, 70, 122
5.23: 2, 5, 15, 17-18, 21, 23, 29-30, 33,
  35-55, 63-70, 72, 77-9, 83-5, 89-91, 95,
  99-103, 110, 114
5.23-24: 7, 24, 30, 32-3, 35, 42, 43, 69, 99,
  110
5.24: 2, 5, 9, 11, 13-5, 21, 26, 30, 33, 35,
  37, 39-44, 46, 48, 49, 65-6, 77, 79, 84-6,
  88, 90-2, 95, 97-8, 100-6, 108-10, 112,
  114-5
5.25: 10-1, 14, 17-8, 27, 51-2, 54-5, 60,
  63-4, 85, 109, 114
5.25-27: 37, 53-4, 60, 91
5.26: 60
5.26-27: 53-4, 63, 95
5.27: 60
5.28: 10, 17-8, 31, 55, 114
5.28-29: 37, 46, 55, 64
5.28-30: 46
5.29: 17-8, 55
5.30: 17-8, 84
5.31: 2, 17-9, 46-7, 55, 60, 64, 92, 103, 105,
  110, 112
5.31-32: 2, 15-20, 45-6, 48, 60, 63-5, 72, 89,
  95-6, 103, 105, 108, 110, 113, 115
5.32: 60, 105, 110, 112
5.33: 10, 32, 114
6.1: 27
6.4: 27, 32
6.5: 27, 31
6.7: 30-2
6.8: 32
6.9: 27-8, 32
6.10: 88
6.10-20: 88, 90, 107-8, 123
6.11: 88
6.12: 88, 91, 94-5, 106
6.19: 83

Phil.
2.6: 12
2.6-11: 56
3.17-21: 52
3.20: 50-2
3.21: 27, 106

Col.
1.15: 75-6
1.15-18: 71, 75, 119
1.15-20: 62, 75-6, 81, 83, 101
1.16: 86
1.16-17: 75-6
1.18: 50, 65, 67, 70, 74-7, 79
2.8-15: 87

2.9-10: 50
2.10: 50, 67, 70-1
2.11: 87
2.12: 87
2.13: 62, 87
2.15: 106
2.18: 67
2.19: 47, 50, 65, 67, 70-1, 73-5
3: 105
3.18: 7, 27-8, 30-2, 50, 66, 92, 97, 105
3.18-19: 7
3.19: 10
3.23: 30-2
3.18-4.2: 6, 30, 37, 70, 122

1 Thess.
1.10: 52-3

1 Tim.
1.1: 52
2: 111
2.3: 52
2.9-10: 111
2.9-11: 111
2.9-15: 30
2.11: 97
2.11-12: 10
2.11-14: 18, 46
2.13: 94
2.13-15: 111
2.14: 94, 111
2.15: 111
2.18-15: 37
4.10: 52

2 Tim.
1.10: 52

Tit.
1.3: 52
1.4: 52
2.1-10: 37
2.5: 97
2.9: 27-8
2.10: 52
2.13: 52
3.1-6: 27-8, 30
3.4: 52
3.6: 52

Heb.
2.8: 106

136 GENERAL INDEX

TIPOGRAFIA POLIGLOTTA DELLA PONTIFICIA UNIVERSITÀ GREGORIANA
PIAZZA DELLA PILOTTA, 4 - ROMA